Dame Vera Lynn was born Vera Margaret Welch on 20 March 1917 and adopted the stage name of Vera Lynn at the age of eleven. She was already an established singer in 1939, but during the Second World War had enormous success with songs like 'We'll Meet Again' and 'The White Cliffs of Dover'. She continued to have a successful career after the war, hosting a variety TV series in the 1960s and '70s. In 1975 she became a dame, and was awarded the Burma Star in 1985. In 2016 she was appointed Member of the Order of the Companions of Honour for her services to entertainment and charity.

Virginia Lewis-Jones is Dame Vera Lynn's daughter. She was born in 1946 and for a time accompanied her mother on tour. She has had many careers, including working in a fashion house, working for Warner Bros Records in California, and as a researcher for the BBC, where for many years she worked on various shows including *Parkinson*, *Crackerjack* and the royal concerts. She now has her own complementary therapy business, alongside running her mother's music company, and is the vice-president of the Dame Vera Lynn Children's Charity. Virginia lives with her husband in East Sussex.

KEEP SMILING THROUGH

'I was just twenty-seven years old when I went to Burma. It was an experience that changed my life for ever. Up until that time, I had not really travelled anywhere at all, apart from one touring visit to Holland with a band I was singing with before the war, and I had certainly never been in an aeroplane. But I wanted to make a difference, to do my bit.' Written with her daughter, Virginia Lewis-Jones, this is the story of the time Vera Lynn spent with troops in wartime Burma. Based in part on a diary she kept, alongside unpublished personal letters and photographs from surviving veterans and their families, it explores why this was such a life-defining event for her, and how her presence helped the people who heard her sing.

VERA LYNN
AND VIRGINIA LEWIS-JONES

◆

KEEP SMILING THROUGH
My Wartime Story

Complete and Unabridged

CHARNWOOD
Leicester

First published in Great Britain in 2017 by
Century
London

First Charnwood Edition
published 2018
by arrangement with
Century
Penguin Random House
London

A catalogue record for this book is available
from the British Library.

ISBN 978–1–4448–3896–1

Published by

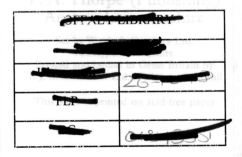

A Mother's Prayer

Only a Mother's Prayer
Whispered in the silence of the night
Only a Mother's Prayer
For her boy who has joined in the fight
Dear God keep him safe from all harm
Wherever he may be
And if it be Thy will
Send him back to me

He answered his country's call
Left home, his loved ones and all
To fight for all he held most dear
Our precious heritage of liberty
So dear God in Thy great mercy
Look down from the Heavens above
Guard him, and send back to me the boy I
  love
This is a Mother's Prayer.

Rosaline Hopkins
1944

Contents

Contents

It is timely that a biography is written on Dame Vera Lynn. We of The Burma Star Association and all the men and women who served in Burma from the Royal Navy, British, Indian and other armies, and air forces, all hold Dame Vera in great esteem and affection as a young lady at the time. She put up with all the hardships and dangers of Burma to entertain as many as possible with her wonderful songs. This gave us all a feeling that we were not forgotten in the Second World War. We were all so pleased that Dame Vera was awarded the Burma Star Campaign Medal.

The Viscount Slim,
President, The Burma Star Association

Introduction by Dame Vera Lynn

As I sit and write this, I have reached the grand age of a hundred. Yet I was just twenty-seven years old when I went to Burma in 1944, and it was an experience that changed my life for ever. Up until that time I had not really travelled anywhere at all, apart from one touring visit to Holland with a band I was singing in before the war, and I had certainly never been in an aeroplane; but I wanted to make a difference. And when in early 1944 I said that I wanted to go overseas, I was determined to do it in a way that most benefited those troops who had not had much in the way of musical entertainment up until that time during the war.

It turned out that the obvious place for me to go was Burma — where the Fourteenth Army had also become known as the 'Forgotten Army'. I think and hope I made a real difference to the thousands of men I sang for in the few months that I was there. And one of the reasons was this very fact: that many of them felt they had been forgotten, and that their effort was not being recognised at home. Of course they wanted to hear me sing, but there was a far deeper need that they wanted satisfied as well — they wanted to renew their emotional connection with home, a place that seemed so far away in every possible sense. For them, I was that connection.

The travel was not like travel became after the war. I did not just go to Burma: on the way I stopped in Gibraltar, Egypt, Iraq and India and saw things that I had never even dreamed of seeing before. For me it was much more than a tour to sing to the troops; it was a personal odyssey that changed me for ever.

Looking back on my long and eventful life, I felt that I wanted to record this important part of it in much more detail than I have done before. I have needed some help to do it, which is why my daughter Virginia (or Ginny, as she is known by almost everyone else) is writing this book with me. It is not just my story, but the story of the thousands of servicemen — who I always think of as, and still call, 'the boys' — who saw me in Burma, who helped me get there and back, and who looked after me in trying conditions that I was unused to. Ginny, who once worked as a researcher at the BBC, made an appeal in the newspapers in 2012 to ask if any readers had stories about seeing me sing in Burma. The response was overwhelming, and we were flooded with hundreds of fantastic letters. She has carefully sorted through them all, and in this book has cleverly brought those stories to light, giving a wider background to what I did in Burma, describing what the boys who listened to me thought and felt when they heard me sing, and telling the bigger story of what was happening in the war at the time.

Introduction by Virginia Lewis-Jones

I've always known that my mother's trip to Burma in 1944, two years before I was born, was a particularly significant episode in her life. But to my mind there has always been something slightly enigmatic about it too. She has written that 'Sometimes I think that I never quite got over that period of my life. My memories of the wartime years are strongest when I think of Burma.' The slightly odd phrasing (why did Ma never get over it?) was in some ways a bit of a mystery to me, and I've never been entirely certain why Burma stood out so uniquely for her, given that the wartime years were memorable for her in so many other ways — she became hugely successful, she sang for Princess Elizabeth at Windsor Castle, she got married, and she met many celebrities, for instance.

Maybe, I thought, it was the strangeness of being in Asia for the first time and the attention she would have received being literally the only woman in camps sometimes consisting of as many as 6,000 men. She told me recently that 'It was so foreign — it was only something like a war that could have taken me there, to a place that was so different to what I expected at home.' But it was only after I made the appeal in the newspapers in 2012 for stories of Ma's tour that something else occurred to me. Perhaps at the heart of it was the sheer emotional power, bordering (yes, really) on delirium, that her songs — and even her presence — created amongst the men serving out

3

there that stayed with her for the rest of her life. Here's just a taste of that passionate response, from a letter written in 1944 by Lieutenant Corporal Ted Lindsay from Burma to his sister in London: 'We went mad, never have I yelled, bellowed, hollered or clapped so much before. I've always yearned to see Vera, always had that ambition and, glory be to me, here she was. I literally went mad.' Later on, he writes that 'I saw, believe it or not, blokes crying with joy at seeing our own Vera.'

Leading Aircraftman H. S. Pewitt wrote to Ma soon after he saw her in Burma with a short piece of poetry he had penned:

VERA LYNN — AN APPRECIATION

Tonight I saw an English girl
And heard the maiden's golden voice
She sang sweet songs of love to me
And made my homesick heart rejoice

Tonight I left the Indian heat
And breathed sweet English air again
The maiden's voice transported me
'Twas home! And I was there again

Tonight of this dear English girl
This message from my heart I send
But yesterday you were a voice
Tonight you are indeed a friend

In our modern age, in which we can communicate instantly with anyone across the world, it is hard to imagine how removed from home it was possible to feel on the other side of the world just seventy years ago. My mother spanned this gap: as this part-time poet wrote, she mentally transported the men back home, if only for a little while, before most of them were sent back to the worst conditions imaginable to fight a brutal war in the jungle. I don't think it is any exaggeration to say that the impact her presence had on the men was like an epiphany — an emotional lightning bolt that struck them as they listened to her songs. The reaction was recognisable from the emotional appeal that Ma's songs had had on listeners since the beginning of the war. For instance, she always remembers a 'middle-aged listener' who wrote in an issue of the *Radio Times* in 1941: 'I can only confess that if 25 years ago that young soldier of an earlier generation could have heard Vera Lynn singing to him — and as if to him alone — simply and sincerely, all the silly insincere songs about home and the little steeple pointing to a star and the brighter world over the hill, that old war would have been made so much the less unhappy for him.'

So Ma's singing had that effect on people in the forces all over the world during the war, but her actual appearance in Burma seemed to amplify it a hundred times. And something quite magical happened there. Her simple but heartfelt songs and her humble and unassuming manner gave reassurance and succour to thousands of young men who were not only terribly homesick but who feared they might never see their homes again. She was the single emotional conduit to home for them, and I think that her appearance in the jungle felt to many like that of an angel dispensing love and hope to those boys who had not in recent times received enough of either of those precious things.

5

She was known before she left for Burma as the 'Forces' Sweetheart'; but some of the soldiers who wrote to her from Burma suggested different names, including 'Sweet-heart of the Jungle', 'Frontline Sweetheart' and 'Sweetheart of the Fighting Fourteenth'. One of these letters even suggested that she should rank alongside Joan of Arc! The letters that the men wrote form an important part of this book. Some were written at the time, in 1944, and my mother kept them in a file at home, along with some of the photographs in this book; others were written much more recently, after we put an appeal in the newspapers asking to hear from servicemen who had memories of Ma's tour, along with more photos from men who had fought in Burma, their children and grandchildren. Both sets of letters have helped in recreating what happened and in getting an understanding of what the tour meant to the men of the Fourteenth Army.

They also help to underscore the fact that this book is far from being just about my mother's experience; it is also about the men she was singing for. I am proud to help my mother tell her story, and the story of some of those men who fought in one of the most challenging conflicts of the twentieth century.

'That's Easy: Burma'

Vera

There I was, in the middle of the jungle, singing my heart out into a microphone, a generator helping to project my voice into the surrounding hills full of tangled unknowns, with my pianist Len pounding a small piano on the back of a truck and me perspiring in the heat and humidity and flapping at the insects that seemed to be buzzing all around me. At the same time, I saw the faces of the boys below me and felt that at that moment in time there was nowhere I would rather be than here — as close to the fight as it was possible for me to be, expressing my own gratitude for what those troops were doing out there, risking their lives every day and enduring for months and even years those same conditions that I had to put up with for only a short time. In that moment I did not worry about the heat, the bugs or the enemy soldiers who could not have been very far away; I simply concentrated on the songs and sang them with as much feeling as I could.

It is rather hard for me to remember, but I did have a life, and, indeed, a successful career, before the Second World War started. I realise that this has not always been the popular idea of me: 'The Second World War was started by Vera Lynn's agent,' joked one comedian in the seventies, for instance. Although my career was well established by the time war broke out, it soon became clear that my songs especially appealed to the time and to the servicemen fighting in the war — something, I think, to do with the emotion that I'd always tried to get across in my singing; what other people have described as my sincerity. I think that was the foundation for my success, and in order to tell the story of how I arrived in Burma, it's important to first of all tell you a little something about my life before the war.

It seems remarkable to me now, but I was born over a century ago, in 1917, while the First World War was still taking place and in the same year as the Russian Revolution! I grew up in the twenties and thirties in a working-class family in East Ham, east London. My mother, Annie, was a dressmaker and my father, Bertram, did all sorts of jobs, including working on the docks, plumbing and glass-blowing. My father was an easy-going man who liked to laugh a lot — and he was also an excellent dancer. Family has always been very important to me — and remains so now — and I was lucky to have a happy childhood surrounded by lots of extended family members — like Uncle George and my grandma Margaret, who both loved to sing. Margaret was my mother's mother, but on my father's side there was also a lot of musicality, with regular sing-along parties at his mother's house on Gillett Avenue and my aunt playing the piano. We often used to go to the East Ham Working Men's Club, where my father was

10

master of ceremonies at Saturday-night dances.

I also used to go to the East Ham Palace with an older girl who lived across the road from me on Ladysmith Avenue. We would pay threepence to sit on the hard seats in the upper balconies, or 'up in the gods', as we always called it. One singer I saw there especially sticks in my mind. She was called Florrie Forde, and I suppose I was about ten when I saw her. Some called her 'the Queen of the Music Hall'. She was an Australian who came to London around the turn of the century and became a big star. During the First World War she sang some of the most famous songs of the time, which came to define the music of that period, including 'It's a Long Way to Tipperary', 'Pack Up Your Troubles in Your Old Kit-Bag' and 'Take Me Back to Dear Old Blighty'.

When you think about it, the sentiment at the heart of all these songs chimes with the type of songs that I would sing quite a few years later. Take, for instance, the chorus of 'Take Me Back to Dear Old Blighty':

Take me back to dear old Blighty
Put me on a train to London Town
Take me over there, drop me anywhere
Birmingham, Leeds, or Manchester, well, I
    don't care
I should love to see my best girl
Cuddling up again we soon would be, Whoa
Tidley-idley-iti, hurry me back to Blighty
Blighty is the place for me.

11

This was not really a war song; it was about trying to hang on to the relationships and people that are important to you while war is all around. The songs I would sing were also about this, so it seems to me, and whether I knew it at the time or not, Florrie was a big influence on me. In fact, she kept singing for many years; she actually died shortly after singing for troops in Aberdeen in 1940.

Given this background, it's hardly surprising that I started singing, although looking back on it now, I don't think it would have happened without my mother pushing me forward. She was the one who wanted success for me and she had it in mind for me from when I was very little — my father, by contrast, was much more laid-back. I first started singing regularly for audiences as a solo performer when I was seven years old. My mother used to design my stage costumes for me — all silk, satin, sequins, net skirts and bodices. It surprises some people that I began singing in clubs at such a young age, but given my background, and the fact that people told me I already had a distinctive voice, I don't think it's so strange. Over the next few years I would sing in working men's clubs all over the East End — from Newington Green to East Ham, Poplar to Stamford Hill. Sometimes I went further afield, to south London and places like Woolwich and Plumstead. I don't remember what I sang that first time I performed, aged seven, but I do know that I was naturally attracted to sentimental ballads, even in those early years, and I had a knack of bringing tears to the eyes of my audience — in the right way, of course!

I was not particularly enthusiastic at school, in part because I had already decided — certainly by the age of eleven — that I was going to be a professional singer and that was that. I remember thinking to myself when I was meant to be learning French, 'Why do I need to learn French when I am going to be a singer?' But it is also true that I was not particularly good at the academic subjects — I struggled with spelling; I couldn't add up; and I was not much good at remembering facts in history and geography. I did like some of the more practical subjects, like art, sewing and cookery. One thing that makes me laugh about school now is that they disliked my singing voice so much that they only let me sing on the front row of the choir because I opened my mouth so wide and it looked good! I have always had a relatively deep voice and everything at school was pitched too high for me, so I usually sang in a horrible falsetto voice. What it all meant was that by the time I was fourteen, I was eager to leave school and start on my singing career. I think I probably rather regretted that later, as I would have loved to have learned more, and for many years I had something of an inferiority complex around clever people (and I have met a great many).

When I left school, I was ready to start as a professional singer, but while I got established, I thought it might be a good idea to earn some money during the day as well. The labour exchange sent me to a little factory in East Ham to sew buttons, but I was already miserable by lunchtime — you weren't allowed to talk to the other girls and I had to eat my sandwiches in a poky little back room. I decided that evening that I wouldn't go back the following day. When I told my dad, he asked me how much I had been paid for the day's work. 'Six and six,' I told him — that is, six shillings and sixpence — 'and not for the day, but for the entire week.' 'Why,' he replied, 'you can earn more than that in one concert.' So I didn't go back the next day, and I never regretted it.

It is difficult to understand now, but bands in those days were booked for all kinds of events, from weddings and birthday parties to company balls and private and public dances. This was long before jukeboxes or music that could be pumped through public address systems — up until the age of fifteen, I had never even used a microphone. A chance encounter led to me starting work with one of these 'gigging' bands — the Howard Baker Band in east London. I was booked to do a cabaret spot in Poplar Baths — a bath house used for concerts and events in the winter months. The Howard Baker Band was booked to provide the dance music that evening, and I realised that it was a big chance for me to prove myself, but unfortunately I had come down with a cold. Added to this, I was asked to use a microphone for the very first time. Well, despite the fact that I had never used one before, and the fact that my bronchial tubes felt as though they had a thick layer of rust on them, I didn't do too badly that night, and Howard

Baker took me on as a vocalist with his band. It felt as though the gate had opened; now I could quite legitimately claim to be a professional singer, and I could charge ten shillings a performance.

Howard Baker had started as a cornet and trumpet player, but he soon realised that there was a high demand for bands all across east London. It meant that he had not just one band, but many of them — sometimes up to a couple of dozen would be playing in different locations on a single night. Those bands gave me both an opening in the music business and an apprenticeship in the finer arts of being a performing artist. I learned how to use a microphone and how to hold myself on stage. Up until then, I had acted out my songs dramatically; now I had to stand still. I discovered that singing with a microphone meant that I lowered my volume and found it easier to sing in lower keys, and my relatively low pitch became an instantly recognisable part of my style.

Two years later, I received my first press notice, a headline in the *East Ham Echo* that shouted: 'STAR IN THE EAST — East Ham's latest contribution to crooning' — a description of my singing that I may not have been entirely happy with, but at least I was getting noticed! When, in 1934, just before I was seventeen, I started singing with Billy Cotton's band, I felt even more that I had made 'the big time', earning the then magical sum of five pounds a week. Stints with other popular bandleaders Charlie Kunz and Bert Ambrose followed over the next few years — and it was during these years that I really began to establish a name for myself; I lost count of the number of times I was told during the war that servicemen had first seen me while I was performing with one of those bands. I earned good money, bought myself a car and a house, and loved being a singer — for me, the music was a constant joy. But above all these things, being a member of the Ambrose Orchestra provided me with the most important meeting of my life — with Harry Lewis, the man who would become my husband.

Harry joined the Ambrose Orchestra in the late summer of 1939 as a clarinettist and tenor saxophonist. We were busy preparing to take our stage show on the road in those months before the war, and although I had noticed the small, dark, handsome man with an impressive head of hair who had been playing with us, it took some time — and much persistence on his part — before I realised what a big role this man would play in my life. It so happened that we had performed together in one of the Howard Baker bands a number of times, but we had never spoken before. It was only when Harry joined Bert Ambrose's band that we really noticed each other for the first time.

After we left Bert's office that afternoon, he suggested that we get a cab together. I told him, rather frostily: 'No, we won't, I'm going on the bus.' That didn't deter him; he climbed on the bus with me and offered to pay my fare. 'I'll pay my own, thank you,' I replied. However, he clearly had his heart set on me. Very early on he announced, quite confidently, 'I'm going to marry you!' I expect that I laughed at that, but we soon developed a closeness that grew and grew. When you spend time in a touring band, you form an intimacy of sorts with everyone in the band — you will either be close friends or bitter enemies, but never strangers. It did not take long for Harry to be the person I would always sit next to on the coach.

In the winter of 1939, while we were doing a week at the Brighton Hippodrome, he said to me again, as he had by that stage done many times, 'I'm going to marry you,' but this time I replied: 'Yes, you are.' However, it took another eighteen months before we actually did get married, on 11 August 1941. Much had changed in this time: the war had started in September 1939, Harry became part of the RAF's 'No. 1 Dance Band' — the Squadronnaires — and I became a famous solo artist in my own right.

A big reason for my growing fame arrived soon after war had been declared. In the autumn of 1939, I came across a song written by Ross Parker and Hughie Charles called 'We'll Meet Again', a song that I have been associated with ever since, and which I never tired of singing. When I first saw it, the words seemed to me to be the perfect example of what I would call a greetings-card song — a basic human message that people want to say to each other but find too embarrassing to actually put into words. Ordinary English people don't on the whole find it easy to express their feelings, even to those closest to them. Not only was the message in

'We'll Meet Again' an important one, and one that I believed in sincerely, I also felt that I could articulate the emotion of the song in a meaningful way to the listener.

We'll meet again
Don't know where
Don't know when
But I know we'll meet again some sunny day
Keep smiling through
Just like you always do
Till the blue skies drive the dark clouds far
*   away*

As more and more servicemen began to move away from their homes in the autumn of 1939, and the future became increasingly uncertain for all of us, the message of the song seemed to mean a great deal to people. And when I went to Burma in 1944, the sentiment at the heart of 'We'll Meet Again' especially touched the men, who had been away from their wives, girlfriends, mothers and fathers in some cases for many years.

The song was a hit, and two further songs soon after were also successful — 'Goodnight Children, Everywhere' alluded to the evacuation of children from the cities, and 'When the Lights of London Shine Again' reflected the fact that our city was now shrouded in darkness at night-time thanks to the blackout. By January 1940, a piece in the *Daily Express* claimed that I was selling more records every month than both Bing Crosby and the Mills Brothers, while in

March the same year my name appeared at the top of a list of favourite female vocalists sent in to a daily newspaper by the men of the Tank Corps. It wasn't that long until I was being called 'the Forces' Sweetheart', and it was a name that stuck.

The radio was a big thing in the war — all kinds of people would gather around the wireless set to find out the latest news — and it turned into a big thing for me too, especially when I started doing my request show in 1941. It was in the form of a letter addressed to the boys, and my sign-off at the end — 'Sincerely Yours, Vera Lynn' — gave the show its name. After the first programme, there was such a flood of mail that we realised that we had struck exactly the right note. More important still, I began to understand just how strong the radio link was. Although we did the programme from a studio, I always tried to imagine myself singing and talking from my own home and addressing myself not to an audience in the conventional sense, but to scattered individuals — an intimate conversation, but to a couple of million people, or however many it was.

Since this seemed to have worked, it made sense to take it further and deliver more personal messages. I thought that rather than being a remote presence on the radio, I should actually step out of the wireless and take that idea of having a conversation with individuals literally. For me, the obvious next thing was to begin to visit hospitals where servicemen's wives had just given birth. I would then broadcast the news and let the lucky man know on the airwaves that he now had a son or a daughter, and that I was there, with his wife, giving her a bunch of flowers and having a cup of tea and a chat. It always felt like such a fantastic thing for me to be the bearer of good news. I imagined the joy those boys must have felt in some far-flung place like Burma or India, mixed no doubt with a little sadness that they could not be there in person.

This I soon realised was more than just a way of communicating with my audiences — it got to the heart of who I was as a performer. I was at my best when I expressed an emotion that two people recognised as a message from one to another. In that way, I came to understand that during the war I helped people to have some sort of emotional conversation over long distances. A song is a dramatic expression of emotion — it often contains the kind of words that we wouldn't say in everyday life, and I'd like to think that those songs helped people to speak to one another in a heightened way. Other people have told me that my songs were a kind of glue that helped people to stay together during those difficult times when a wife would not see her husband sometimes for years.

Yet although there was a lot of popular appreciation of my songs, there was also a significant minority — mainly politicians and high-ranking retired military officers — who thought that my music was sentimental slush and that it should be taken off the BBC. They objected because they felt that fighting men should be listening to fighting music rather than songs that made them think of home and the loved ones they had left behind. I felt the opposite to be true, and I received plenty of support from the boys I sang for in this.

★ ★ ★

I remained in London for most of the war years. I drove my little green Austin 10 with a soft top through the Blitz and often got caught in the blackout. There were times when I was performing at the Palladium and I got stuck there all night waiting for a raid to finish. You would put a metal plate over your car headlights with a little pinhole in it so that you could see other drivers in the distance — and they could see you. I used to carry a tin helmet with me on the passenger seat, and if I got caught in a raid, I just put it on and drove on.

Harry and I finally married in August 1941. I had just recovered from acute appendicitis after collapsing and then being carried off stage at the Palladium in July of that year, while I was performing in the show *Applesauce*. I was operated on immediately. I made a good recovery in the Essex countryside, and just a few weeks later, on 11 August, Harry and I got married at Marylebone registry office, along with about two dozen guests — mainly just family. We took a five-day honeymoon in Paignton, Devon, and made sure to take our ration books with us — even in hotel restaurants, they would tear out the coupons for your food. After that, I returned to the Palladium, resuming the *Applesauce* show.

I sang in other places around the country, sometimes performing with Harry's band. On one occasion, in 1942, I was doing a week's variety at the Sunderland Empire when I was called away for a special performance for the royal family at Windsor Castle. The occasion was the then Princess Elizabeth's sixteenth birthday. What a treat that was — to sing for the future Queen in her own home! But early the next morning I set off for Sunderland again to resume my tour of variety theatres, munitions factories, hospitals and recording studios.

I could have gone on like that for the entire war, alternating between London and performances around the country — Coventry, Glasgow, Wolverhampton, Edinburgh — but there was one thing I hadn't done, and as time went by, I became more and more acutely aware of where my next duty lay. It may seem strange to say, but I suppose it felt a little futile, reaching out only on the radio and in shows around the country, and not, or so it seemed to me, actually supporting the men overseas who were fighting the really hard fight and putting their lives on the line. Quite simply, I wanted to help do my bit, and, as far as I could see, that meant heading abroad.

To do my bit on the front line I needed to join ENSA — the Entertainment National Services Association — which had been set up by Basil Dean in 1939. Basil knew lots of people in the entertainment business and had himself been an actor, writer, film and theatre producer and director. Before the war he had set up Associated

Talking Pictures, which later became Ealing Studios — the legendary production company probably most famous for those wonderful post-war comedies like *Kind Hearts and Coronets, The Love Lottery* and *The Ladykillers*, starring people like Alec Guinness and David Niven.

Basil had established ENSA with Leslie Henson — another actor turned theatre and film producer — to provide entertainment for the troops. It was part of the Navy, Army and Air Force Institutes (NAAFI), which ran the clubs and canteens on the military bases where the performances would often take place. With so many servicemen spread around the world on hundreds of bases, it was a tough job entertaining them all, and I'm sure it's true that the talent got spread a little thin at times, which led to the rather unkind nickname for ENSA in the forces — 'Every night something awful!' But looking back now at the list of names who performed on behalf of ENSA, it's amazing to see the quality of the stars — some at the start of their careers, others as established members of the entertainment scene. They included people like Jack Hawkins, John Gielgud, Gracie Fields, Vivien Leigh, Spike Milligan, Alistair Sim, Noël Coward, Joyce Grenfell, and my great friends Elsie and Doris Waters — the double-act known as Gert and Daisy. And I don't think that you could call any of that list second-rate.

So there I was, walking down Drury Lane one morning in early 1944, and at that point I don't think I could have had any idea that this very ordinary walk through London's West End, of the kind I had done hundreds of times before, was actually the beginning of a much more momentous journey halfway across the world; a journey that would remain with me for the rest of my life. The truth is, I never meant particularly to go to Burma — like most people, I expect, I didn't know much about what was going on in the Far East, and I had no idea that this was where I might be needed the most.

In London, we were mainly concerned with the state of the war with Germany, and especially with the bombs that had been falling on the city since the start of the war, though far less frequently than at the height of the Blitz. By that time, with the Germans having been chased out of North Africa in 1943, inroads being made into Italy by the Allies in early 1944, and the Soviets gaining ground all the time, it felt that the tide was turning in Europe. Of course, we all followed what was going on in Europe avidly, and every day the papers and the wireless broadcasts would report the latest victories. But things were rather quieter about what was happening in the Far East, largely, I suppose, because we hadn't been doing so well out there. I certainly remember hearing about atrocities in POW camps — the foreign secretary, Anthony Eden, made a speech about it in the House of Commons in January 1944, which began with the words: 'I fear I have grave news to give to the House.' He went on to detail the way in which Allied prisoners were being tortured and starved in camps and to warn the Japanese government that their maltreatment of prisoners would not be forgotten. There was a lot of anger in the country about this, but I still did not know at that stage the difference between Rangoon and Imphal, the Arakan and Assam.

I doubt very much that I was thinking about any of these things as I sat down in Basil's little office in the Theatre Royal. I remember that there were lots of mirrors and ENSA posters for entertainment nights on the walls, a large black typewriter on the desk, and a sign that said 'YOU ARE SPENDING SOLDIERS' MONEY' in capital letters. Basil, who was in his fifties, with thinning hair, a smart suit and black-rimmed glasses, looked over and asked me straight away where I had thought of going.

'Well,' I said, 'the troops in Italy and the Middle East seem to be doing all right as far as entertainment goes, so if I'm going, I'd like it to be where I can do the most good, where not many performers get to.'

'That's easy,' he said. 'Burma.'

He told me that not that many entertainers had made it out to Burma — Noël Coward, comic Stainless Stephen, music-hall duo Gert and Daisy and comedian Joyce Grenfell, as well as a handful of others, but that was about all. He asked me to consider it, but I didn't need to — for me it was an easy decision, which looking back on it now seems slightly strange. I had only been married to Harry for two years and I have no idea what he thought of it — I never thought to ask him! But in any case, he would not have tried to stand in my way. In fact no one tried to dissuade me from going, even though in many

25

cases I was going to be the only woman among thousands of men, singing near to the front line in the most primitive conditions imaginable. I am still not quite sure why I felt I had to go there, but I knew that I had to get as close as I could to the actual fighting. For me, this meant going to meet the troops in person; it meant doing everything I could possibly do to support them and let them know that back in England we were all thinking about them and willing them on.

The next thing I had to do was more practical — I had a busy schedule for the following few months, and my agent, Leslie McDonnell, had to find a way of clearing it. Against his better instincts — good agents always try to gain bookings rather than cancel them — he succeeded, and between March and June 1944 I was free to travel to Burma.

Ginny

I am always amazed at how carefree Ma sounds when she talks about heading off to the front line in Burma when she had only once been out of the country before — and that was just across the Channel to the Netherlands, and in peacetime! I was not yet born at that time — I did not come along until 1946 — but I know that my father, Harry, who is sadly no longer with us, would have supported Ma in everything she did.

It seems hard now, at a distance of more than seventy years, to fully understand the risks that she was taking, but I believe they were significant. The obvious danger was that she would get caught up in the fighting, or be captured by the Japanese. This was a real possibility when you consider how close she eventually got to the front, and the volatile nature of the military situation at the time. Yet she had well-founded faith that she would be looked after by the servicemen that she was going to be singing for: 'Of course I didn't feel scared — I had six thousand men to look after me when I was closest to the front,' she would often tell me, with a smile on her face, as though she never had a single doubt that she would be fine.

In fact, she probably faced a far greater risk from contracting illnesses like malaria, dysentery and typhus; many more soldiers were receiving treatment

27

for conditions such as these than they were for injuries that they had sustained fighting, and mortality rates were far higher than they would be today because methods of both prevention and treatment were more primitive. There was also an arduous multi-leg journey on many planes to consider, and general conditions in the jungle — heat, humidity, basic living arrangements and an austere diet — that would be no different to those faced by men hardened by training and years of living amongst it.

The situation in Burma was in the balance at the start of 1944. Up until that point, British forces in South East Asia had not inflicted a defeat of any significance on the Japanese. In fact, the Allied forces until that point had been largely humiliated, and their morale was suffering.

During 1941 and early 1942, the Japanese army had driven Allied troops out of Burma. They were a formidable enemy — they had become expert in moving through the jungle, and they fought with bravery and infamous ruthlessness to the extent that in some quarters they had, worryingly, acquired an almost supernatural reputation. Their tactics were also aggressive and bold. General Slim, who commanded the Fourteenth Army, wrote of the Japanese soldier that 'He fought and marched 'til he died. If five hundred Japanese were ordered to hold a position we had to kill four hundred and ninety-five before it was ours — and then the last five killed themselves. It was this combination of obedience and ferocity that made the Japanese army, whatever its condition, so formidable, and which would make any army formidable.'

In 1943, the Allies attempted an offensive into the

Arakan, the western province of Burma. It was a catastrophic failure: many of the units were poorly trained, unable to cope with the trying conditions and prone to suffering from tropical diseases. They also failed to cope with Japanese tactics, which relied on infiltration rather than full-frontal assaults. The defeat in the Arakan created a dangerous and precarious situation for the Allies. As Ma left the Theatre Royal and walked out onto Drury Lane after meeting Basil Dean, she may have looked down the road and seen India House, the High Commission of India, on Aldwych, just a couple of hundred metres away. The very real threat at that exact moment in time was that the Japanese would soon invade India and establish an unassailable position across the Asian theatre of war.

Back in August 1943, Winston Churchill, with the agreement of the Combined Chiefs of Staff, had decided that a change in leadership was needed in order to try and reverse Allied fortunes in Burma, and so a new Allied Supreme Command was created for South East Asia with Lord Mountbatten at its head. And it was Mountbatten's decision, in October 1943, to choose General William (Bill) Slim as the commander of what had previously been known as the Eastern Army, but which from then on was called the Fourteenth Army.

Slim has since been credited as one of the best commanders of the Second World War, and a pioneer of modern warfare. He and my mother, who first met one another in Burma, would remain great friends for the rest of his life. According to Robert Lyman, one of the general's most distinguished biographers, 'Slim was one of the pre-eminent soldiers of his generation. Tough, wise, accessible to all, he was the epitome of

29

the great commander. Physically imposing, Slim had a prominent square chin that gave him a look of purposefulness and determination. His physical appearance was not deceptive. Slim, against the most formidable of obstacles, helped to transform Allied fortunes in Burma.'

In 1944, when Ma first met him, Slim was fifty-three years old and held the rank of lieutenant general. Like Ma, he came from a relatively humble background: his father worked in the wholesale ironmongery business in Birmingham, and before he joined the army at the outset of the First World War, Slim himself had been a teacher and a factory clerk. At the start of the Second World War, he had commanded the 10th Indian Infantry Brigade of the 5th Indian Infantry Division in East Africa, before moving to the Middle East, where he commanded an infantry division and was twice mentioned in dispatches in 1941. He moved to Burma in March 1942, and his eighteen months of operational experience as a corps commander before he took over the Fourteenth Army gave him a valuable opportunity to assess the strengths and weaknesses of the Allied forces.

The Fourteenth Army contained over half a million men, who between them spoke twenty-eight languages. It might technically have been a British army, but it was ethnically and religiously extremely diverse: it contained, among others, Gurkhas (from Nepal), Indians, West Africans and Burmese Karen tribespeople; Hindus, Muslims, Christians and Jews, all of whose contributions were important to its effective operation.

After his appointment at the head of the army, Slim

quickly identified that even before crafting an effective strategy for warfare, there were four main challenges he needed to overcome in order to begin to change the fortunes of the Allies. The first was to find a way of mastering the local conditions — the dense jungle, the heat, humidity, high rainfall and lack of infrastructure — which made fighting a war there extremely difficult. He wrote: 'The individual soldier must learn, by living, moving, and exercising in it, that the jungle is neither impenetrable nor unfriendly. When he has once learned to move and live in it, he can use it for concealment covered movement, and surprise.' The second challenge was to improve his troops' training; the third, their health; and the fourth, their morale, which had been sapped not just by the series of defeats but by the terrible conditions they had been fighting in. It is hard to be optimistic when you have malaria — and up until autumn 1943, a staggering — so staggering that I had to double and triple-check that this was right — 84 per cent of front-line soldiers contracted the disease in India and Burma, though it affected different servicemen to varying degrees.

Poor health and disease was more than merely an inconvenience and an impediment to effective warfare; it was actually an existential threat to the army. Slim later wrote: 'At this time, the sick rate of men evacuated from their units rose to over twelve thousand per day. A simple calculation showed me that in a matter of months at this rate my army would have melted away. Indeed, it was doing so under my eyes.' The other remarkable statistic that Slim gave is that, at this time, for every man evacuated with wounds, 120 were evacuated sick. I think this

31

demonstrates just how serious the health issues were and the dangers that my mother potentially faced in going out there.

Slim, who was a highly pragmatic man who paid meticulous attention to detail, took practical steps to address the first three of the major challenges, and felt that by so doing, the fourth — the morale of the troops — would improve in turn: mastering the conditions and improving training and health was bound to make the boys feel better about their prospects. He saw the poor morale as like a disease in itself. 'Many became contaminated', he said, 'with the virus of despondency.' Poor health, heat, humidity and a ferocious enemy were all factors, but what made it worse was the fact that many in the Fourteenth Army felt that they were fighting a forgotten war. According to Slim:

> The British soldier, especially, suffered from what he felt was the lack of appreciation by his own people and at times their forgetfulness of his very existence. The men were calling themselves a 'Forgotten Army' long before some newspaper correspondent seized on the phrase. After all, the people of Britain had perils and excitements enough on their own doorsteps and Burma was far away. Its place in the general strategy was not clear, nor did what happened there seem vital. Much more stirring news was coming out of Africa. It was no use belly-aching because the Fourteenth Army was not in the headlines of the home papers; so far, we had not done anything to put us there. When we had won a victory or two we should be in a better position to complain. All

the same, this feeling of neglect, of being at the bottom of all priority lists, had sunk deep. There was a good deal of bitterness in the army, and much too much being sorry for ourselves.

Probably the best boost to morale, as Slim observed, would come from starting to change the momentum of the conflict, and in February 1944, the Fourteenth Army gained a small but significant victory in the bloody Battle of Ngakyedauk, often also called the Battle of the Admin Box. 'It was a victory', wrote Captain Anthony Irwin, who took part in the battle, 'not so much over the Japs but over our fears.' It also suggested tactics that could be used to defeat the Japanese in the other battles that were yet to come.

This battle took place just a few weeks before my mother flew out. It may have had a galvanising effect on the boys, but morale was still fragile in March 1944. Captain Woodcock, serving in the RAF in Burma, wrote that 'Operationally, the beginning of February [1944] was a fairly quiet time and the monotony was relieved by a visit from Lord Louis Mountbatten on the 8th. [. . .] News from home was infrequent and newspapers almost non-existent. Combined with the weather this was a most depressing time.'

One of the big problems faced by servicemen in Burma was the lack of contact with home — there was no telephone, and letters took weeks to arrive. Clearly, the fact that so few entertainers came out to the troops was also a contributing factor to the sense of being cut off from home. Slim himself complained that before my mother, and others, went out to the Far East in early 1944, 'the stars of ENSA were as distant and aloof as their celestial counterparts', confirming Basil Dean's sales pitch to Ma in Drury Lane that this was where she was needed the most. I think the fact that Slim, the commander of the army, thought it worthy of comment shows that he understood the operational value of entertainment as a means to help raise the general morale of the troops.

Slim became affectionately known as 'Uncle Bill' in the Fourteenth Army, and has been described as a man with 'the head of a general and the heart of a private soldier'. He understood that the men serving under him were not machines; they needed emotional and spiritual nourishment as much as bully beef and bullets. In his characteristically thoughtful and disciplined fashion, he took some time to define his own ideas about morale. I repeat them here because I think they capture something that is at the very heart of my mother's mission to Burma:

> Morale is a state of mind. It is that intangible force which will move a whole group of men to give their last ounce to achieve something, without counting the cost to themselves; that makes them feel they are part of something greater than themselves. If they are to feel that, their morale must, if it is to endure — and the essence of morale is that it should endure — have certain foundations. These foundations are spiritual, intellectual, and material, and that is the order of their importance.

I'm fairly certain that Ma didn't think about her singing to the troops in anything like these terms, but she did understand, I think, that she raised the spirits of the men she sang for, and gave them hope and joy. More than anything, I believe, she gave them a connection with what Slim called the 'part of something greater than themselves' — in particular, the idea of home and everything it meant. This was something that had become tenuous for many of them; some soldiers had not been home for years, and had few reminders of it out in the jungle. Sergeant Major H. Jackson of the 17th Indian Division Signals wrote to Ma in 1944 to say that 'I have been in the forward areas nearly three years and getting a little tired of it all now, still it cannot go on forever.' Another serviceman called Jimmy Reed also wrote in a similar vein:

Four-and-a-half years in India has done me little or NO good. The last time I had the extreme pleasure of seeing you was at the Palace Theatre, Manchester, with Ambrose and his band in September '39, just before I had the misfortune to be sent abroad, and listened, midst all the comforts possible at home, to yourself and Jackie Cooper singing 'You Can't Black Out the Moon'. I got more pleasure out of that performance than anything else that happened to me since I first set foot in India.

As Ma readied herself for her journey to Burma, new battles were about to begin — like those at Kohima and Imphal. These took place over almost the exact dates that she was in the country, and together they turned out to be the most significant turning points of the entire campaign. I like to think that my mother being there gave the troops a really important boost at

35

this decisive time. Of course it would be too much of an exaggeration to say that she made a vital difference in helping to change the course of the war in South East Asia, but I like to think — and I think it's realistic to suggest — that her contribution did give the servicemen strength, courage and belief that they had not been forgotten — and that this renewed their determination to fight.

My mother may not have realised before she left how close she was going to get to the front line, but in the end she got very close, probably just a handful of miles away and certainly close enough that Japanese soldiers hidden in the jungle in the hills above would have been able to hear her sing. I sometimes wonder what those soldiers might have thought as they sat in their foxholes and heard the piano and Ma's voice echoing around the hills and through the dense tangled undergrowth . . .

But hold on a second, I am leaping too far ahead — first she had to get to Burma, and her journey was not the straightforward flight that it would be today; instead it was an epic trip across a war-torn world.

Flying Boats and Pyramids

Vera

I turned twenty-seven on 20 March 1944, but while I celebrated my birthday, I had my mind on other things. I was excited and nervous about my journey, and I had to keep it a secret too, which made the excitement and nervousness all the greater. Just three days later, on 23 March, I put on the rather stiff and bulky ENSA uniform — a knee-length pleated skirt, a stiff jacket with black and white ENSA motifs sewn into the shoulder seams, and a matching cap — and set off on the first leg of my journey. Only one person would travel with me for the whole trip, a man who would be my faithful companion and accompanist throughout: the great pianist Len Edwards.

Len was a little older than me and had played piano for me a number of times before. He didn't have any particular style that I can remember; he just accompanied me very well and allowed me to express myself exactly as I liked. Obviously I had to take someone with me who had worked with me before, so that they would know what key to play in and how I sang. ENSA paid a small fee of twenty pounds a week, which I passed on to Len — I never took any money for entertaining the troops, as I saw it as a duty that I was happy to do for nothing.

I carried with me one object as I left for foreign shores that I was not strictly supposed to have with me — a little burgundy Collins diary in which I wrote tiny, terse, cryptic notes that even I afterwards struggled to understand! I think I wrote in this way so that if the diary did fall into enemy hands (the reason why I wasn't meant to have it in the first place), then they wouldn't understand it either. But however difficult it may be to read, it has certainly helped me to piece together some of the memories from all that time ago.

We started our journey inauspiciously, according to my diary — the first leg took us to Swindon. From there we headed to somewhere on the Dorset coast — I don't remember where, but probably Poole, I imagine — and soon after midnight the next night, we took off for Gibraltar in a Sunderland flying boat. It is not exactly how a plane journey in a passenger jet might be these days — there were none of the soft seats and air conditioning. Travelling in general in the war was a particularly austere experience, and you have to remember that Len and I were to spend almost all of our time on transport that was meant for carrying servicemen. Of course I had plenty of experience travelling with bands before the war, in coaches crammed full of musicians and instruments; but those trips seemed the height of comfort compared to the various journeys we would endure over the next few months. Quite honestly, I did not mind a bit of hardship — I had expected it, and I always felt that whatever I had to endure was nothing compared to what the average soldier, sailor or airman had to put up with.

The flight to Gibraltar was my first ever flight, and I think it would be an understatement to say that I didn't enjoy it: I was airsick the entire time. It wasn't that I was nervous; it was just that I had an upset tummy. It was like going to sea for the first time, and the weather wasn't all that good. The aircraft had two decks; I spent most of my time on the lower deck, where there were bunks, a galley and, most importantly, a flush toilet. As the crow flies, it was not a long journey, but at that time it still wasn't possible to fly through occupied France and (technically) neutral Spain. It meant that we had to first of all head west, as though we were going somewhere towards the Americas, and then, in the middle of the ocean, turn in a big arc towards Gibraltar. It took seven hours in all.

The civilian population had been evacuated from 'the rock' at the start of the war, and Gibraltar had become a fortress guarding the strategic gateway to the Mediterranean. We stayed there all day and I took the opportunity to send some parcels home and buy some bananas — the first I had seen since before the war. Then, just after midnight, we were off again, past the many searchlights that probed into the darkness, looking for enemy planes. We flew first to Castel Benito airport outside Tripoli, in Libya, where we had breakfast. Tripoli had only been taken a year ago by the boys of the Eighth Army, and it wasn't until May 1943 that the Italians had been kicked out of North Africa entirely.

After breakfast we headed on to Cairo, where we arrived at 1.30 in the afternoon. I think we were meant to stay at a hotel called Shepheard's, but alarmingly there had been some insect infestation there. I cannot remember exactly where we did go in the end, but I have some notepaper from the Continental Savoy on Opera Square, so I think we must have stayed there. This grand hotel had had its fair share of illustrious guests, including T. E. Lawrence ('Lawrence of Arabia') and Lord Carnarvon, who had opened the tomb of Tutankhamun and soon afterwards died in the hotel from a mosquito bite infection, leading to speculation about 'the curse of the mummy'.

It was only later that I learned that at the same time I had been travelling to Cairo, General Wingate, leader of the British special operations group in Burma, the Chindits, had been killed in a plane crash. I met many of the Chindits when I made it to Burma, and they spoke highly of him. I gathered that Wingate had also stayed in the Savoy in Cairo, back in 1941, and, while suffering from malaria, had unsuccessfully tried to kill himself in his hotel room. It turned out that my short stay would be rather less eventful and traumatic.

I was tired and disorientated by all the travel, but our hosts immediately whisked us off to see the pyramids and the Great Sphinx of Giza, just outside the city. I enjoyed the excursion, in spite of my tiredness: what remarkable and ancient monuments they are, and what a privilege it was to be able to see them.

Then the next day, quite to my surprise, the owner of the hotel we were staying in whisked us off to the races! I had never been to a race meeting in my life let alone put on a bet, so I was quite astonished when I walked away from the race track having backed four winners and with an extra thirty shillings in my pocket!

Egypt wasn't just a stopover on the way to Burma — I performed there, and in a number of other places along the way as well. It was in Egypt that I first got a taste for the type of performance that I would be doing during the tour. People suggested for many years afterwards that I had travelled with an elaborate wardrobe of costumes. The very opposite was true. I had taken one dress — a pretty, flowing pink chiffon number, which, as it turned out, I would barely use. I could only really wear it indoors, and most of my performances would be in the open — something I had rarely done before. But it did occasionally come in useful and I think the boys appreciated it. By the end of the trip I felt rather sorry for it — it suffered terribly in the heat and humidity!

My first performance of the trip was in the desert at El-Qassassin. There I sang in a sandstorm for 3,500 men of the Royal Artillery who had just returned from fighting the Germans on the coast of Italy. We had intended to do the show in the open, in front of all the men, but the sandstorm made that impossible. Instead, I did three separate shows in two marquees. The conditions were pretty awful for singing, and in retrospect I wonder if this was one of the causes of the problems I would have with my voice once I reached Calcutta a few days later. As I stood in front of the boys assembled in that first marquee, the wind was swaying the structure and letting in great blasts of sand through the base and sides. It got everywhere — in my ears, nose and throat — and I struggled to see my audience in the thick fug, let alone make myself heard. I was then ferried through the storm to the second marquee, where a new set of men were assembled waiting for me, while they cleared out the first marquee and gathered the third crowd of the day. I think they appreciated that it was not an ideal environment to sing in — or listen to music in, for that matter — but they seemed so thrilled to see me and had even baked a large cake with the words 'Welcome Vera' on the top. Sadly it got smothered in sand and ruined.

After the concerts, I went back to Cairo, where we stayed for just one more day. One highlight was going to the amazing Khan el-Khalili bazaar, where I bought some shoes as well as an 18-carat-gold ring watch that cost the princely sum of 1,400 Egyptian pounds, from a shop called 'J. Bossidan: Oriental Jeweller, Curios & Silks' — I know this because I still have the receipt! Sadly, I don't know the whereabouts of the ring watch; my feeling is that I gave it to somebody as a gift, but I can't remember who! That is the problem with reaching the age of a hundred — however much you would like to remember things, sometimes it simply is not possible. The bazaar in Cairo was like nothing I had ever seen before: a magical maze of narrow streets bedecked with mirrors, clocks, spices, lanterns, jewellery, shoes, ceramics, gold and statuary. The smells were of dried roses and spices and tobacco, and I suddenly felt that I really was a long way from east London.

The following day, 29 March, we flew early in the morning in an Empire flying boat across the Suez Canal. This was a large (for the time) and bulky-looking aircraft, not dissimilar to the Sunderland flying boat I had started out from England in, but without the guns fitted to it. The weather was bad and we had to make use of the fact that we were in a flying boat when were forced to land on the Dead Sea. Here I experienced the torture of airsickness and seasickness at the same time. But we soon took off again, flying across the biscuit-coloured desert of Iraq and landing on the Euphrates River alongside the RAF station at Habbaniya, between Ramadi and Fallujah.

After a short stop there, we carried on, following the mighty river down to Basra, just below where the Euphrates and the Tigris meet to form one great wide brown stream. Bad weather stranded us there for longer than expected — on 31 March, we were awoken in the painfully early hours to only be told that we couldn't fly. We did eventually take off, but the weather forced us to turn back again. I ended up doing some impromptu singing at a supply base before we had a lovely dinner at Colonel Mole's mess. My diary reveals that I was in bed by 9.30

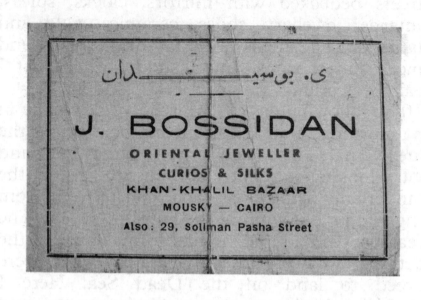

ی . بوسیــــــدان

J. BOSSIDAN

ORIENTAL JEWELLER
CURIOS & SILKS
KHAN-KHALIL BAZAAR
MOUSKY — CAIRO
Also: 29, Soliman Pasha Street

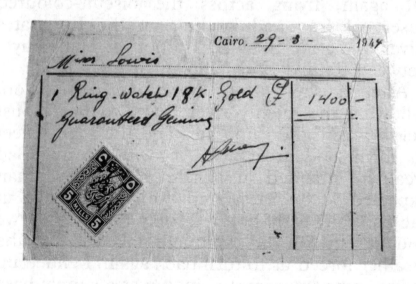

Cairo, 29 - 3 - 1944

Miss Lewis

1 Ring - Watch 18 K. Gold 1400 -
Guaranteed Genuine

that night, ready for another attempt to leave early in the morning.

The first day of April began early once more, and we left Basra at 3.50 a.m., heading first for Bahrain, where we had tea and sandwiches, and finally reaching Karachi, which was then in India. We were made very welcome there in the mess of the Somerset Regiment. One of the RAF boys who had been doing a similar journey to me recently wrote in a letter: 'What a day to arrive in India — April Fool's Day 1944.' The rest of the letter gives a bit more detail:

So you were a day late in arriving in India — but at least we almost had dinner together!

I had completed my operational training at 730 TU Abu Suweir in Egypt at the end of March 1944 — on P-40 Kitty-hawks. Such pilots were not required in Tunis or Italy so 'they' decided to send us to India to convert onto other aircraft. Myself and three others were the first to be posted there and went to El Maza to board an Imperial Airways Ensign to make the journey.

Late in the afternoon we landed at Basra to be told that a severe sandstorm 'over the gulf' would prevent progress and we would have to stay the night at the Shatt-el-Arab Hotel. It seems that you were making a similar journey in one of the flying boats using the river on the north side of the hotel and airfield. The point being that we dined in the hotel's restaurant (I recall it had mirrors on the walls and columns and seemed endless). And there, seated at an adjacent table, was our favourite singer from her days with the Ambrose Orchestra, Vera Lynn. No, I didn't ruin your dinner. Nor did you invite me for a brandy. But at least we almost had dinner together — then what might have resulted!

The following day we went on our way — you to the India-Burma area to the gratitude of the troops there. Me — to remain at Karachi for a start and to learn to fly other aircraft and, eventually, over to the active area.

So much nostalgia of those distant days, much sadness and a few bright memories. At least I'm lucky to have survived — and I'm told that I should write a book too.

Unfortunately, I was not able to see Karachi properly, as we stayed on the base before heading off to Bombay the following day, so I had not yet got a proper taste of India, but the following day I certainly did.

We continued in a land (rather than sea) plane. After a delay due to the wheels getting stuck in the sand, the plane set off, and by 6.30 p.m. we had arrived in Bombay, where we stayed at the grand Taj Mahal hotel. Almost the first people I bumped into there were Elsie and Doris Waters. Meeting them in the Taj Mahal hotel in Bombay felt no different to meeting them backstage at the Metropolitan on Edgware Road — they were just ordinary, nice people.

Ex-BBC manager Eric Dunstan, now with the rank of colonel, was the ENSA man in charge in Bombay, and he sent a note to the hotel to welcome us to India. I still have that note.

Dear Miss Lynn,
 I cannot leave Bombay to welcome you to India myself but Lt Stewart is my substitute. We are delighted to have you and hope we can keep you for a long time. I've made no definite plans to meet you which I felt was wiser than committing you to plans which might not work.
 Thank you for coming.
 Yours sincerely
 Eric Dunstan

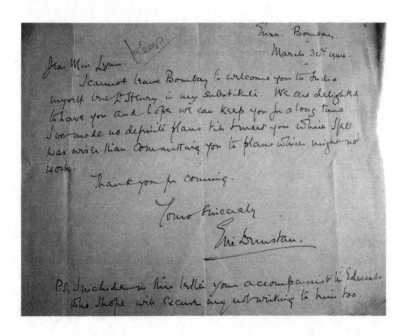

The work really began on 3 April when I did an open-air show at a transit camp, a concert at a nearby leave camp and a show at the YMCA. I also found time to have my hair done before moving on to Calcutta on 6 April.

I hadn't enjoyed the flying, but what seemed to make it even worse was the early starts — up early once more, our next move in a Lockheed Hudson, a twin-engine light bomber. This brought us, by way of Nagpur, to Calcutta, which was where many of the men who had been fighting on the front line came back to on leave. I would spend a few days there, singing for them and doing other engagements, but in many ways it still felt like a rehearsal for the ultimate mission. My final destination was looming: I was heading further and further east and getting closer and closer to Burma.

Ginny

Ma's journey to India was remarkable not only because of the number of legs involved (seven flights in all from Dorset to Bombay, not including the forced stop on the Dead Sea and the false start from Basra), but also because of her stoicism in the face of an arduous journey and treacherous conditions. When telling the story of leaving for Burma, she does not recount saying goodbye to Daddy before she left — and I think that is representative of her attitude of carrying on without any fuss, as well as of the general feeling of the time: the importance of keeping a stiff upper lip, even when you were nervous, anxious or worried. In fact, my instinct is that Ma was not particularly any of these things; I think she always believed that she would return safely, and this was part of the aura that she projected to the troops, and which they loved so much.

My mother may have believed that she would be looked after in Burma and that everything would be organised for her, but there is no doubt that she had to endure discomfort. This is of course a relative thing — especially during wartime — but flying clearly didn't agree with her. One wireless operator called Dan Webb, who flew with 238 Squadron, remembered one leg of Ma's journey when he wrote to her in 2012. 'You flew in our DC3,' he wrote. 'When you felt queasy, Bruno, the pilot, told you to 'chuck'

51

downwind. Bruno is dead now. I was the wireless operator with 238 Sqdn RAF. Never forgotten you — you bring tears to my eyes when you sing — still.' When I read this postcard, I couldn't help hoping, because of the way it is phrased, that Bruno didn't die as a direct consequence of my mother chucking downwind!

Despite her nausea, though, Ma stopped for breakfast, tea and sandwiches on the way, as though they were on a day trip rather than a great journey across the world in the middle of the war. To me it enhances the idea that she had just popped out from home to see the boys; to sing her songs and have a cup of tea. She tells me that she remembers one of the boys saying, 'Home can't be that far away, 'cause you're here.' It shortened the distance, which up until the time she came and sang to them had felt so enormous to so many of the servicemen. And when you look at the photographs, she is always smiling, fresh-faced and relaxed and clearly enjoying herself.

In one interview, she said that the idea for her to go to Burma had met with some opposition from the British Cabinet, some of whom, she claims, felt that there was something improper about a woman travelling to entertain so many men on the front line. Her retort was: 'Look, I've been singing in working men's clubs since I was seven years old — I can handle myself, don't you worry.' I don't think that she did have to worry. It may seem easy to say now, but I believe there was a real innocence in the way that the men regarded my mother, which was all to do with her personality, her background and the type of songs that she sang. Rather than being a substitute for their girlfriends and wives, she was a messenger between them; rather than a pin-up idol, she was like a sister and a friend. 'It is quite true, Miss Lynn,' wrote Private Pottrell of A Company, Second Battalion, in Burma, 'that you are beloved quite as much by the girls as the boys.'

The letters Ma got from the boys show this perfectly: they are all respectful and dignified; often they mention a sweetheart left at home — like Howard Withington, who wrote to my mother from 30 Squadron, RAF India Command, in May 1944: 'Is it possible that when you get home to Blighty you could sing 'Apple Blossom Time' on 14 August 1944 for my girlfriend's birthday — Joy Mould of Moston, Manchester?' These were the kinds of requests that she got all the time from the boys. And of course it helped that she had come from a relatively humble background herself — something that she has never forgotten. The regular troops came from the same type of families, grew up in the same kind of streets, and felt that she was 'one of them'.

Corporal Ronald Felton also wrote a letter to my mother, which I think is a lovely expression of this kind of respectful admiration:

Yes it is good to know that you loved the reception we gave you out here when you visited us, the boys and I of the 3rd Tactical Air Force are so pleased that you were happy in giving so good a show to us, for as you know it is a terrible country here what with the heat and transport problems and we are so very proud of you for being so kind as to visit us.

We shall always remember you Vera for visiting us in our hour of need, you are our

'Forces' Favourite' and what a 'Favourite' believe me, your records are everywhere and most days we hear your lovely voice on the wireless so you see clear how the public love your voice and those who have come into contact with you love you for what you are, a very good singer and a charming and understanding lady.

As Ma left Europe, the war was heading in the right direction as far as the Allied forces were concerned, with the Soviets speeding westwards and the British and Americans making progress in Italy. But the overall result of the war was by no means certain, and in March 1944 the terrible bloody Battle of Monte Cassino was still being waged, with the British Eighth Army and the US Fifth Army trying to break through German defences to capture Rome. It would take until May to achieve their objective, at the cost of 55,000 lives. At the same time, although only a few people knew about it, preparations for the D-Day landings were already in an advanced stage; it so happened that they took place on the very day Ma returned home from Burma.

Although the troops in Burma had scored one notable victory in February 1944, at the Battle of the Admin Box, the changes that General Slim had brought in to improve the way his soldiers operated in the tropical conditions — their training, health and morale — were yet to be fully tested. The Battle of the Admin Box did point the way to tactics for future conflicts, though, such as the Battle of Kohima, which began on 4 April, as Ma was in Bombay, and the Battle of Imphal, which had started in March. The nature of the battle and the tactics are worth looking at in a little more detail in order to understand the overall situation in Burma at that time and to give some idea of what the men that Ma would be singing for had experienced — or were about to experience.

* * *

The Battle of the Admin Box took place in the hilly jungle country of the Arakan region of Burma between 5 and 23 February and was so called because the site of the battle was a roughly rectangular administrative area for the Indian Army's 7th Division. This became a defensive position after the divisional headquarters of General Frank Messervy were taken by the Japanese on 5 February with their signature tactic of using a widely dispersed force to attack the flanks and rear rather than a frontal assault. Their next target was the administrative area, which was cut off from Allied support and manned by a variety of defenders, including medical staff, clerks, drivers and tank crews. Given that no defeat of significance had yet been inflicted on the Japanese, this was not the force that Slim would have chosen to fight such a potentially decisive battle for troop morale! He wrote that he believed at the time that the troops within the admin box were 'prepared for nothing more than raids'. Yet at the same time, one of the most significant things that he had been drumming into his troops ever since he took command of the Fourteenth Army, almost six months before, was that 'There are no non-combatants in jungle warfare. Every unit and sub-unit, including medical ones, is responsible for its own all-round protection, including patrolling, at all times.' The value of this philosophy was about to be proven.

The battle that followed involved a great deal of vicious hand-to-hand combat, and some truly terrible things happened — for instance, when the Japanese ran through the medical tent, killing thirty-five staff and patients. The historian James Holland, in his book *Burma '44*, described some of the fiercest fighting:

It was all over for most in the opening minute as the tightly bunched enemy troops were torn to shreds. Some still managed to scramble up the banks of the nullah [Burmese word for a watercourse, riverbed or ravine] and one officer slashed his sword down towards the orderly room sergeant, only for the sword to get caught in the wood of his rifle butt. Pushing the Japanese officer off balance, the sergeant swung around his rifle and plunged the bayonet into the enemy's belly, while a corporal next to him added his own thrust. Others now climbed out of the trenches and pursued those desperately trying to escape.

The men defending the position were courageous and resilient beyond measure, yet they could not have done it were it not for the support of the Allied pilots who dropped food, ammunition and medical supplies into the admin box. This allowed them to break the stranglehold of the siege and effectively nullify the Japanese tactics of encirclement. The Japanese were forced to retreat back into the jungle and the Fourteenth Army had won its first battle, something that Slim rightly anticipated would set the pattern for all future encounters. 'It was a victory,' he wrote, 'a victory about which there could be no argument, and its effect, not only on the troops engaged but on the whole Fourteenth Army, was immense. The legend of Japanese invincibility in the jungle, so long fostered by so many who should have known better, was smashed.'

It also showed that the war in the jungle would be won by a combination of troops on the ground and superior air force — and my mother sang on plenty of RAF bases as well as for the army boys.

After the Battle of the Admin Box, Slim realised that the Japanese would soon be advancing and that the result of the coming battles could be decisive in the overall Asian theatre of war. The hope from the Japanese side was that a march into India would provoke the Indian nationalists into an uprising against the British. Slim, on the other hand, wanted to smash the Japanese troops on the Indo-Burmese border and send them running back into the Burmese jungle with their tails between their legs. In order to keep the initiative and choose the battleground on which to fight, he decided to bring the Japanese army towards the British defences by withdrawing onto the Imphal plain.

The plain was one of the few flat areas in the mountainous region that divided Burma from India. Just over a hundred miles north of Imphal was the railhead and crucial supplies base of Dimapur, and in the hills above this was the small settlement of Kohima, set on a high ridge. The Japanese began marching on Imphal near the start of March 1944, but in addition, they also sent a whole division to try and take Kohima and cut off the British troops at Imphal. Slim had only anticipated that they would send a regiment, and desperately sent for reinforcements. For the next few months, while Ma was touring in India and Burma, the outcome of these two battles would hang in the balance, through some of the fiercest fighting of the entire war.

At the same time as the Battle of the Admin Box had been taking place, back in February 1944, the group of long-range penetration troops known as the Chindits had been parachuted in behind enemy lines to try and disrupt enemy troops, facilities and lines of communication. This was called Operation Thursday. The leader of the Chindits was originally General Wingate; as Ma says, he died in an aircraft accident on 24 March, when the B-25 bomber he was flying in crashed in bad weather. His replacement was Brigadier Lentaigne, and Ma met him as well as many of the Chindits during her time in Burma. They were all trained and expert in moving stealthily through the jungle, and Ma always says that she would be standing in a clearing and they would suddenly appear from amongst the trees like spirits of the forest!

It must have been quite something for my mother arriving in India for the first time. Most of the troops arrived by boat after a far longer journey than that which Ma had made. For those, like her, who had never been to India before, nothing could have prepared them for the sights and sounds of the subcontinent.

Major Mike Lowry, who was twenty-five years old in April 1944, was B Company commander of the 1st Queen's Royal Regiment. He had first arrived in Bombay back in 1939, and stayed at the same hotel as my mother.

I took a taxi to our allotted hotel, the Taj Mahal.
We thought that maybe we were more special

than most, as our taxi flew a Union flag on its radiator; we were soon to learn that there were other taxis which flew the flag, and that the taxi drivers thought that they were all rather special driving around with Union flags and consequently inflated their charges!

We found ourselves in the best hotel, maybe the second best, in India. The Taj Mahal hotel had been converted into an officers' club at short notice; most of the civilians who had been there had to make way for about 1,000 officers who had landed from the Britannic and the Duchess of Bedford.

The hotel gave us a five- or six-course meal that night, followed by cabaret and dancing. We were only there two days and two nights, but we managed to explore some of the city and bazaars. Our senses were really hit as we took in our first impressions of eastern living: the smells were deep, pungent and what to us seemed fetid, and was almost at the same time reprieved by the fragrance of eastern incense; strong though it was, I much preferred it to the stench of feet, BO and orange peel on 'D' deck! During the afternoons and as dusk quickly descended we were staggered to see Indian bodies lying on the pavements, pedestrian islands and almost anywhere; they all looked quite dead, and the more so as their faces were covered with a shroud. We were to soon learn that this was a habit of the continent, the Indians would doss down when and where they felt inclined and cover up their heads to keep off the flies.

Not all the servicemen arriving in India were so enthused by their surroundings. Lieutenant Charlie Bratley was one of those who was less than impressed. 'Well, I've arrived,' he wrote in a letter home in 1944, 'but I wish to goodness I hadn't. Give me England any day!! India simply stinks — in fact I think it's bloody awful. I've been here a few days now, and I'm fed up already. I'll have to try and get used to it, though, as I'm going to be out here for a lot longer spell then ever I expected. I'm afraid it will be all of five years for me.'

It had not helped the morale of many of the troops to find that once they arrived in India, they faced a dearth of good entertainment. ENSA in Bombay may have suffered from its fair share of problems in the early years of the war, but by the time Ma arrived there in 1944, things were improving, and she was leading the way for other entertainers to make the same journey.

The actor Jack Hawkins, who had been commissioned into the Royal Welch Fusiliers, was the British Army's liaison officer with ENSA in Bombay. Celia Nicholls, an ENSA entertainer who was in India during the war, remembered being quite star-struck in his company, but found that he was very charming to all the performers. She recalls that 'We were stationed first of all in the Apollo Bunder Hotel in Bombay and I'm afraid we began to put on weight as we enjoyed all the fabulous meals on the menu, such a luxury after war-rationed Britain.'

Hawkins wrote, rather less cheerfully, in his memoir that 'I don't suppose that even the world's most unsuccessful theatrical agent has ever had to handle quite so many deadbeat acts as were sent to me

60

. . . So far as ENSA headquarters in Drury Lane were concerned, we were not only at the bottom of their catalogue of priorities, we were the bottom.' General Slim was determined to improve this situation. But even in some of the shows that Ma appeared in, some of the men were less than impressed with the other acts. In a letter to his sister, Corporal Ted Lindsay wrote: 'Three weeks ago Matt and I went to an ENSA show; see it was PBA: rotten comedians, fat women with corkscrew-shaped tonsils; we were browned off with it until some chap mounted the platform and said: 'A miracle has happened tonight, boys, here she is, your own sweetheart, VERA LYNN!'' I assume that PBA stands for 'pretty bloody awful'!

My mother did not meet Jack Hawkins in Bombay, but the fact that celebrities of the time like him were organising entertainment for the troops just goes to show that there really was very little tolerance of 'grandstanding' during the war, even if you were a star. Ma was certainly a big star in 1944, but she did not have any kind of retinue travelling with her — just her pianist Len. There was no army liaison, ENSA representative, make-up or hair person; no camera crew, journalists or photographers. She did not take an extravagant wardrobe with her. At many places, she practically rolled off the plane and started singing — there was very little time for her to rest and recuperate. This did catch up with her fairly quickly, however: by the time she got to Calcutta, she had practically lost her voice.

The Lost Voice of Calcutta

Vera

I was already exhausted by the time I made it to Calcutta; I was not feeling my best, and the weather was so hot and dry that I even found it hard to breathe, yet alone do anything else. But I hadn't gone all that way just to lie in bed! So practically the first thing I did when I arrived on Good Friday, which fell on 7 April that year, was to go to a large hospital where many of the wounded boys from the battles in Burma were being treated.

I ended up spending quite a bit of time in hospitals on my tour, and each visit would take a long time because of course I toured every ward and sat on every bed and chatted with everyone I met. This experience made me understand that talking with the boys, giving them the chance to ask me questions and simply being there for them was just as important as the actual singing part — if not more so. They seemed to enjoy having me there and were desperate to find out more information from home. They could not telephone, so everything they heard was from newspapers, letters and the radio. And all of those things are pointedly not conversations — you just get given some information but you cannot ask any questions (and the round trip for letters was often about six weeks). So I was always asked, touchingly, 'How are things at home?' I say touchingly, because all the boys were worried about their loved ones' safety — despite the fact that they themselves were in hospital being treated for wounds and disease! Because I had travelled around so much in Britain — from Sunderland to Brighton and from Cardiff to Crewe — I always asked where someone was from and tried to tell them about something I had seen in their home town. I let them know that things were all right — that we were holding our heads up and carrying on as usual.

Straight after that first hospital visit, we went to a gun site on the outskirts of town. But whether it was because of the change in temperature, the sand in Cairo, or just fatigue — or a combination of all three — my voice had faded badly. I wrote in my diary that evening: 'Lost piano. Mike broke down. Voice very bad.' It wasn't a good day — all the travelling had got to me already and I had only just arrived. Things didn't improve the following day either. I wrote in my diary that 'I can't speak and can't breathe.' I felt that it was the atmosphere — it was suffocatingly hot and dry — and I was worried about the fact that my voice had gone. I'd come out to entertain the boys and the first thing that happened to me was that I lost my voice and I thought, 'That's a bit unfortunate, to say the least!'

My pianist Len also had an asthma attack and had to go to hospital, and we had to cancel the show that night. I couldn't sleep because the noise of the hotel laundry below my room and the bites of the insistent bed bugs kept me up all night. Fortunately, a lovely man from ENSA called Major Jack Bontemps came to my rescue and put me up in his bungalow to spare me the bites and the noise. On 9 April, we had a free day and so I sunbathed in the garden and tried to get my voice back. That evening I had dinner at the very grand Government House in Calcutta with dignitaries including Richard Casey, an Australian who was the Governor of Bengal, and Hawthorne Lewis, the Governor of Orissa, as well as their wives and various representatives from the army.

I only had one day of relaxation, as I was to join an ENSA concert party called Smile Awhile on the 10th, who were based in Barrackpore, to the north of Calcutta, which had up until recently been the Burma HQ. My first performance with them also turned out to be my last — some of the

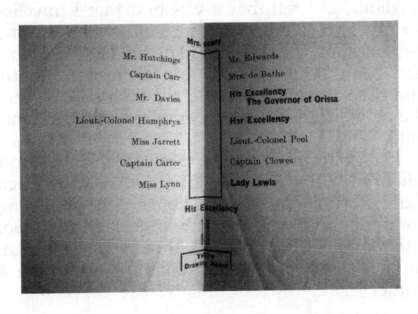

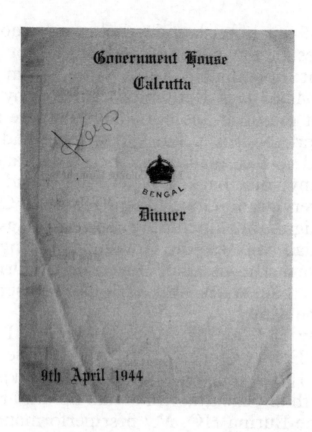

Government House
Calcutta

BENGAL

Dinner

9th April 1944

cast seemed to resent my coming fresh out of England, so I felt that it was best that I travelled on my own. I didn't enquire as to the reasons, but perhaps they didn't like the fact that they had been slogging away out there for months and then I came and stole all the limelight from them, which would be completely understandable.

The following day I received a note from Major Melling of the Royal Army Medical Corps, who was clearly concerned about my condition and warned me that I should look after myself differently, as threats to well-being in the east were rather different to those at home.

Dear Miss Lynn,

I am sending herewith a bottle of medicine for you but I would advise that you see a doctor today as you will appreciate that the laws of health are more stringent in this country than at home even and a slight neglect of yourself now may result in a prolonged period of illness later on.

Apart from this matter, I would like to thank you personally for your help in the show last night which, in addition to its intrinsic charm was, in all the circumstances, a very courageous effort. Thank you very much indeed.

The circumstances he was referring to were those of my struggling voice, and of course I did try my best to sing in spite of the fact that what came out was not always what I intended! His warning, as it happened, did turn out to be something of a prophecy, as on my return from Burma I did indeed suffer a 'prolonged period of illness', basically because I was completely exhausted.

The day after that show, on the 11th, I was back in Calcutta, signing records for soldiers in a funny little gramophone shop in a narrow alley. I was kept busy the following day with filming for a newsreel, alongside a broadcast and then a live show in aid of the Indian Red Cross. I still have the letter, from a 'P. de Peterson', confirming the booking:

Captain Ross Parker has told me that you have very kindly consented to appear on the

Red Cross Radio Variety Programme on Wednesday the 12th instant.

I would like to take this opportunity to express to you the thanks of the Indian Red Cross society and the St John Ambulance.

Our programmes on the air are a comparatively recent addition to the work being done in this province, and I am convinced that your appearance will give us the type of publicity which we so badly need.

On the 13th, I did a show at the Loretta Convent Hospital — made distinctly memorable because of the number of snakes that made walking a precarious business!

It has been said many times before, but it is a small world, and during the war it seemed especially so: with people moving about all over the place, you would always bump into someone you knew. Captain Ross Parker, mentioned just above, for instance, happened to be the writer of two of my most famous songs — 'We'll Meet Again' and 'There'll Always Be an England'. I met him on my way back through Calcutta on my return from Burma, a meeting I'll tell you about later on in the book. While I was out in the East I also came across a number of people from my part of London whom I had either known before the war or who were familiar with Ladysmith Avenue and Upton Park and other places in my neck of the woods. I also received letters while I was there, like this one from George Gilbert-Davis, an old acquaintance who was now in the British Army.

I was amazed to read in the papers that you were in Calcutta, only I have just left there and during my stay in Calcutta I was always hoping you would come. But as such luck happens, not until I have left the !!!! place.

Well Vera! How are you, and your folks? Has your mother come out with you to keep you company? Or have you had the luck to join your husband?

Yes, I know I am all questions, but you see I have been out here two years now without seeing anyone I really know, and I feel very excited to know you are here. Before you came abroad, did you see anything of my wife? You remember her don't you, you met her many times with me, at 'The Royal Oak', Faircross [Barking]. By Jove! I can see that saloon bar now, serving up the old 'Taylor Walkers' beer.

How is your brother Roger and his wife? I do hope things are well for them. The last time I saw him he was in the RAF. Has he had to leave his wife and come abroad? Oh! How I should love to see you, to talk of old times, and hear all the news. And by the way I have not forgotten the beer you promised me, I'll keep you to that if ever I get the opportunity to see you out here?

I heard from old Ben Gilbert about a week ago, he is now in North Africa. Times have changed since the club days, haven't they? Do you ever think of the times at the East Ham Club? And Stamford Road Club? I have never heard how Les or Phyllis are, I don't think I have seen any of them since the war started. Gracie (my wife) is still in Ilford (about five minutes from your house) and is still keeping her chin up, but is finding it more and more difficult to do so. As for myself, I am afraid I get the blues, and it is very hard to jump out of them.

Now Vera! You must write to me, and tell me what you think of India and the 'black hole' of Calcutta. Please tell me of the tips you had coming across, were you sick? Or full of the joys of spring?

It was lovely to hear a voice from home, and I wrote back to my old pal to let him know how I was getting on in India. He was not the only local lad out there, and one of my brother's friends, Sergeant Dawson of the Royal Engineers, also got in touch to say hello.

It was a grand surprise to learn of your intended visit, and your arrival, hoping to have the chance of seeing you once again, the last time being when at Ladysmith Avenue, so long since.

Your brother Roger, Dougie Boggis and I worked together at Newtons, if you can remember back as far as this, and it was with them that I first made your acquaintance, so I trust you can find just a few spare minutes of your precious time to enlighten me on Roger's present whereabouts.

There are several locals in the company,

from East Ham, Barking, Plaistow, just to mention a few, and 'hot' news from home would certainly be appreciated.

The mess extends a hearty greeting to you, if by good fortune, you could arrange a flying visit.

Hoping you are finding India to your liking, and await your esteemed reply.

You have to remember that in those days, people wrote letters all the time. My brother, Roger, and my husband, Harry, were both back at home. Roger was working as ground crew in the RAF, servicing aircraft, and Harry was touring the country with the Squadronnaires band. He didn't pass the medical for combat because of his bad sinus problems, which later forced him to give up his musical career as well. I wrote to him a number of times while I was away, but other than missing him, I don't remember that I was particularly homesick — I just wanted to feel better so that I could get on with what I had gone out to India and Burma to do.

I had a busy few days the following week, singing at hospitals and RAF bases. On 17 April it was two shows at Le Martinique Hospital in the morning and one at an ack-ack (anti-aircraft guns) site. On the 18th there was a big thunderstorm as I made my way to sing for 176 Squadron on the outskirts of Calcutta. It was probably the most terrifying thing that had happened to me since the Blitz! The following day I did two shows for 155 Squadron, one of the first squadrons out in the East to receive Spitfires, at the

73

start of the year. The boys seemed to be enjoying the shows and I got a number of letters from servicemen thanking me for my efforts. Joseph Hines, a leading aircraftman in the RAF, originally from Bermondsey in south London, wrote to me on the 15th.

> It was certainly grand to see and hear you sing once again.
> This is the first time that I have seen you for three years, and I felt very happy when I read that you were coming out to this country, and was hopeful that I would be able to see you, and tonight I will be seeing you for the third time, I bet that my folks back home will be jealous when I tell them about it, as like myself they are all big fans of yours.
> I certainly picked the right time to come to Calcutta on leave, and now after hearing you sing I can say that I have had an enjoyable leave.
> I wish that Lord Winterton was out here to see the reception that you have received wherever you have gone, and I think that he would have had to agree that the boys do want to hear you, and believe me we certainly do.
> When we read his article referring to you in the paper, well I don't know what we weren't going to do to him.

Lord Winterton was a Conservative politician who had criticised my singing and suggested that the men needed some sterner music in order to prepare them for fighting. 'I cannot believe that all this wailing about lost babies can possibly have a good effect on troops about to engage in a very serious pursuit in which their lives will be in danger, and who are about to take part in some of the biggest operations we have ever seen,' he had said in the House of Commons in March. He also seemed to think that German radio was 'infinitely better than ours'. I did not pay too much attention to his criticism, but it was nice to know that I made a difference to the people that really mattered to me — the servicemen I was singing for.

Signalman Shearing heard me sing on the 10th in Calcutta and wrote to me the following day to also offer his support: 'I did hear it said

India.
May I take this opportunity of voicing the appreciation of thousands of servicemen who had the pleasure of hearing Vera Lynn when she gave a terrific performance at a hospital in this area. If only Lord Winterton could have been there, and heard the cheering and whistling for encores every time Vera tried to leave the platform, he would have been forced to change his mind about female crooners and the morale of the troops.

I say emphatically that the morale of the troops went up 100 per cent after hearing Vera sing.

that the BBC had banned you from radio as your sentimental way of singing was bad for the morale of the troops. Well here's one guy you can quote anytime — my morale was boosted 200 per cent last night.'

My voice was much better, but that problem had been replaced by others — there were endless tummy upsets, about which the less said the better, and I also got the prickly heat rash so famed in the tropics that many of the soldiers also suffered from. But for a few days from 19 April I did have some time to myself, and I managed to relax a little and do some swimming. I had been able to swim ever since someone pushed me into the pool when I was at school and I doggy-paddled to the side, and — other than on that very first occasion! — it has always been something that I enjoyed and found relaxing. In the heat of Calcutta, it was especially soothing, and I began to feel a little more acclimatised to the conditions that had been such a shock to my body when I first arrived.

In Calcutta, I still felt a kind of underlying restlessness — I was on the way to my ultimate destination, which was as close to the front line as possible, to see the troops who were trying to stop the Japanese invading India and push them back into Burma. The next stage of that journey began on 22 April, when I headed from Calcutta towards the front line, flying in a postal delivery plane that dropped the mail at two places along the way. And in the act of doing something as mundane as delivering the post, I felt as though I was heading into the unknown.

Ginny

In the minds of some of the troops — like that of Sergeant Major Jackson of the 17th Indian Division Signals — Bombay may have been 'the nearest place to dear old England' that they would see in the subcontinent. However, Calcutta, in the eastern corner of the country, close to what was then the border with Burma, was where most of the supplies for the front came through, and where most of the servicemen spent their leave. It was also a major medical centre for troops who had been injured or taken badly ill in Burma. April, when Ma arrived, is one of the hottest months of the year in the city, as the temperatures build before the monsoon rains arrive in June.

As the commander of a force of half a million men, Slim was not just responsible for his men's ability to directly wage war; running the army also meant providing food, shelter, healthcare and entertainment, as well as the logistics behind the provision of all these services. It meant that in effect he also had to be a road builder, a farmer, a medic, a caterer and a compère. One of the greatest challenges was getting supplies to the front line in Burma, made especially difficult by the inhospitable terrain on the Indo-Burmese border. Most of the supplies were taken from Calcutta by train, then unloaded and put on a smaller narrow-gauge railway. The next stage involved crossing the vast Brahmaputra River by boat, before getting on another train. Finally, trucks would complete the journey by road. Some indication of what this journey involved is given by Captain Ian Wallace, who was serving in the Royal Artillery.

On the 29th January 1944 at 11 p.m. I started my journey from Calcutta to the Arakan. No lights were provided so torches were at a premium; however, we were all provided with bunks and had a comfortable night. There was a certain air of tension, as for most of us it was our first move into action and Chittagong seemed veritably the front line. We reached the Brahmaputra ferry at ten o'clock the following day and spent the next very pleasant day steaming up the river and contemplating the future. Excellent meals were provided on board and we succeeded in securing a berth on the Chittagong train in the evening. The Brahmaputra seemed, and I suppose was, an immense river. At time the banks were hardly visible and the distance between the banks must have exceeded ten miles. All types of exotic native sailing craft were plying up and down and occasionally we passed other steamers or barges.

The roads in Burma were rudimentary, and so the army engineers — as well as a force of 40,000 local labourers — had to build miles and miles of new ones, using bricks that were made in specially constructed kilns at regular intervals along the newly built highways. These roads had to be tough enough to withstand the monsoon rains that would turn dusty tracks into quagmires. This was all part of Slim's gargantuan effort to supply the front-line troops with everything they needed to wage effective war.

Amongst those supplies was an enormous amount of food. As Napoleon is reputed to have said, an army marches on its stomach, and without enough food it would be impossible for the Fourteenth Army to fight effectively. But trying to cater for half a million men needing three meals a day and comprising a variety of nationalities and religions, including both Hindus and Muslims, was an enormous undertaking. There were thirty different ration scales to cater for the different needs of the men. Much of the food came from India, but it was also necessary for the army to produce its own — in large part because there was no refrigerated transport, and so any fresh produce being transported by train would quickly turn to rotting mush in the hot carriages. As Slim's son, Colonel John Slim, said to me: 'If you have nothing, you improvise,' and so they did.

Slim and his most senior administrator, Major General Arthur Snelling, set about growing their own vegetables on 18,000 acres of land, rearing sheep and goats and running duck farms for meat and eggs. The scale of the operation was truly remarkable. Food actually turned out to be one of the decisive factors in the Battle of Kohima, and shows how important planning is in military matters — as far as possible, nothing can be left to chance. Snelling acquired the nickname 'Grocer Alf' because of the logistics that were required to do all of this. He even managed to set up mobile breweries so that there would be beer for the troops as well!

Snelling had plenty of experience, and his input into the war in Burma should not be underestimated. He was born in 1897 and grew up in Norfolk before

79

enlisting at the age of eighteen, when he was commissioned as a second lieutenant. In the First World War he was in Mesopotamia (now Iraq). Between the wars he remained in the army, serving in Afghanistan, the north-west frontier of India, Burma and Bombay. He also spent time training at the Staff College in Camberley, Surrey. His work in the Middle East in the Second World War gained him significant recognition; this was where he first worked with Slim, and soon afterwards he was given an OBE for his services in Iraq, Syria and Persia. The citation for the OBE praised his 'organising ability, initiative, energy and compendious knowledge of administrative technique'. Once Slim took over the leadership of the Fourteenth Army, Snelling quickly became one of the most important members of his team, and Slim trusted him with the enormous responsibility of feeding the men. 'Snelling's task was an immense one,' wrote Slim, 'and, having discussed it with him and selected the key men to work under him, I gave him a very free hand to carry it out.'

Medical care was also transformed under Slim's watch. In terms of disease, far more emphasis was placed on prevention, especially with malaria, and it was strictly enforced, as Ma would soon find out! This meant taking anti-malarial mepacrine tablets every day, wearing trousers instead of shorts, and buttoning down shirtsleeves at dusk. There was a widespread — and incorrect — rumour that the pills caused impotence, and many of the men refused to take them, but after Slim did a series of surprise inspections and sacked three commanding officers whose men were not taking the tablets, they soon got the message. The number of servicemen contracting

80

malaria quickly began to decline.

One of Slim's key principles in terms of medical care was to treat soldiers as close to the front line as possible. Servicemen who had malaria had previously been transported hundreds of miles back from the front line to hospitals in Calcutta or elsewhere in India. Instead of doing this, the army began to set up malaria forward treatment units (MFTUs) just a few miles behind the fighting lines. It meant that a man taken ill with malaria would be treated within twenty-four hours and would be back fighting again within weeks rather than months. The same principle was applied to the wounded, with field hospitals set up 'almost in the midst of the battle', according to Slim. In the case of the Battle of the Admin Box, back in February 1944, this meant that medical staff and patients were caught up in the action and killed by the Japanese. But across the whole theatre of war, it also meant that many lives were saved that would otherwise have been lost. The situation was further helped by the increase of air evacuations rather than taking the seriously wounded by truck and train. Slim wrote: 'Only those who have suffered the interminable anguish of travel over rough ground or tracks by stretcher or ambulance and the long stifling railway journey for days on end, with broken limbs jolting and temperatures soaring, can realise what a difference quick, smooth, cool transport by aircraft can mean.'

William Savage, a private with the 1st Battalion Devonshire Regiment, experienced both a road and an air evacuation as he was taken off the battlefield at Kohima, and ultimately back to Calcutta, where he was in hospital when Ma came round doing her visits. He wrote in his memoirs:

I was eventually taken to the casualty clearing station on a converted jeep where my left leg was put in plaster . . . When I was in the casualty clearing station the casualties were rolling in, several of my mates were coming in. We were eventually moved from there from one field hospital to another and I'll always remember the small arms fire around us and I almost expected the Japs to come rushing through the tent at any time but it never happened. I was eventually driven back to the Imphal airfield and you can imagine on a rough track with a broken leg how painful that was. After waiting at the airfield for what seemed like several hours, they were waiting for planes to come in and take wounded out I suppose, and I got taken to Calcutta.

While I was in Calcutta hospital, one bright moment was Vera Lynn coming round the wards and singing to the troops. It was one bright moment in our lives.

As an insight into what one of Ma's many hospital visits would have been like, Leslie Munder of the 2nd Reconnaissance Regiment Royal Armoured Corps remembers what happened after he was evacuated from Kohima with a bout of malaria that almost killed him.

Whilst taking part in the Battle of Kohima I contracted a very dangerous form of malaria. I was posted to a medical centre within Kohima. And for three days I was in real danger of dying. My life was saved by a very skilful British medical officer aged about 50 years with many years experience in the medical service. After passing through the most dangerous part of my illness after 4 days I was posted to an Indian General Hospital in the next forward base. [. . .]

The day after I arrived, the ward master of my ward came and smartened the beds and told all the patients: 'You are going to be visited by Vera Lynn.' We were fairly delighted by the announcement. About 10 a.m. Vera Lynn appeared surrounded by a group of officers. There were 36 beds in the ward. Vera stopped and she shook hands with every man, gave him a Red Cross gift, soap, or handkerchiefs etc. and had a few words with each man. When she came to my bed we shook hands, she gave me a lovely smile, and said: 'Where do you come from in the UK?' I replied, 'Not so far from you, madam. I come from SW London before being bombed out and running away to join the army.'

Compared to these matters of life and death, the need to provide entertainment for the troops may have seemed to be low down on the army's list of priorities. Yet Slim understood that Calcutta had to provide servicemen with an opportunity to unwind. He wrote:

The modern British or American serviceman is a townsman, and, especially after a spell in the jungle, he yearns for the once familiar distractions of the city. Calcutta alone in eastern India could offer these. It had cinemas, restaurants, and clubs equal to those of the great cities of Europe, but it offered also less reputable relaxations, running down the whole scale of vice from doubtful dance halls to disease-ridden dens of perversity. The problem was to provide wholesome amusements in such abundance that the soldier would not be lured into these darker byways. In this we got no help from home; we were thrown back on our own ingenuity and on what the civilian community could do to help us — and that, considering their limited resources, was a great deal. To them we owed our first theatrical companies.

As Slim notes, there were very few acts coming out from Europe, so members of Calcutta's British community set up the Bengal Entertainment Services Association (BESA) in 1942, and the lecture theatre of St Xavier's College on Park Street became their theatre. Frank Leadon was a student of the school at the time: 'As a 10-year-old on my evening return from St Xavier's,' he remembers, 'I'd peek in and never forgot the Vera Lynn visit as I was a fan and used to sing her songs at parties in my boy soprano voice.' BESA gave their first performance in 1942, and by 1944 they were giving nine performances a week. Later on in 1944 they would merge with ENSA as my mother and other pioneers helped to establish Calcutta as a fixture on the ENSA performers' circuit.

Although Calcutta may have been a place full of familiar forms of entertainment and relaxation, for many visitors to India, unused to seeing so much poverty and disease on open display, it was still a shocking place to come to for the first time. Catherine Wells, a dancer who toured India with ENSA in 1944, remembered:

Calcutta station appalled me. It was as crowded as the Grand Hotel, but this time with beggars and down-and-outs in the most wretched states of destitution and disease just lying about every- where. It was distressing enough to see them in the streets, pestering for annas outside the Grand Hotel, holding out withered arms or half starved babies, but here they just lay hopelessly, almost as if they were piled up for the dustcart.

You may remember that Lieutenant Charlie Bratley had also been shocked by his arrival in India, writing home to say that it 'simply stinks'. Soon afterwards, though, he was sent to a jungle training camp to learn how to navigate through thick undergrowth and other skills that would allow him, in Slim's words, to understand that 'the jungle is neither impenetrable nor unfriendly'.

Here I am, nicely settled down in my new camp. It's a bit 'rough and ready', and very lonely, but, on the whole, life ain't too bad at the moment. We're living in tents, miles away from 'anywhere'. The food is plain, but good, and there's plenty of it. We have some jolly good instructors, who treat us with great consideration. It's not such a 'battle school' as I expected. The main idea seems to be to get used to living in the jungle, and finding our way in the dashed thing. It's a most difficult job. Two steps without a compass, and you're absolutely lost. Everyone goes around with a compass secured around the neck, a map, and a protractor. Without them it's impossible to do a single movement.
I spent a night in the jungle, away from camp

last week. It was a most weird experience. I had a few million insects, bug, beetles etc. to contend with. The only wild animals I saw were large grey monkeys. They make a fearsome row, specially when I was trying to get some sleep. It's poured with rain every day since I arrived here. I seem to live in a perpetual state of dampness, but it's cured my prickly heat. It's also taught me to keep my matches dry.

There are also some fantastic letters sent to my mother both at the time and more recently that help to bring Ma's time in Calcutta to life. This letter from Signalman Shearing is a particular favourite of mine, as I think it shows how deeply appreciative and moved the boys were by Ma coming out to sing for them in person. I find his enthusiasm extremely touching.

Dear Vera,

Having always been one of your keenest and ardent admirers, I had a very pleasant surprise when you appeared at our camp last night with the ENSA party. This was the third time I have had the pleasure of seeing you in person & you were more wonderful than ever last night, despite the fact you were suffering from throat trouble & I personally want to offer my sincerest thanks for bringing me down to earth & making me realise I am English once more. It was great to see a product of good old Blighty standing out head and shoulders above everyone else. Yes I saw you at the sergeants' ball later on in the evening & if I say you were the belle of the ball that would be putting it mildly.

There is no object to this letter. It's just that I felt I must show my appreciation of your travelling over 6,000 miles to sing for the boys. I put my address at the top, but don't know why, because I know that you are too busy to reply to individual letters. One of your non-admirers here said you would not reply to it, but I put the address there just in case & I'm hoping.

However, I would like to make a much bigger request than a reply to this letter — if I may. You have had numerous requests in a similar strain — I know, because I have followed your wartime career just so earnestly as I followed your peacetime one. I have been in this war since the very first day — heard you sing many times over the air whilst I was in France. During the Battle of Britain I saw you in 'Applesauce' & also at the Services Spotlight at Hammersmith Palais. Having been in India for 3 years, I rate last night's performance as your finest hour — and mine! I am now eagerly awaiting the arrival of your three films.

The request, by the way, that Signalman Shearing was building up to asking for, was for Ma to sing a song on the radio for his mother and 'my girl, Marge'. He particularly requested two slightly older songs from the pre-war years: 'Wishing' or 'The Bells of St Marys.'

Miranda Oliver sent a letter to my mother in 2011 about her grandfather, who had served in Burma. He was in Calcutta at the same time as Ma and apparently was doing some shopping in Calcutta for his three-year-old son (Miranda's father). He had no idea what to buy but fortuitously bumped into Ma on the street and asked for her opinion. She pointed to a canary-yellow suit, which he bought on the spot and sent home to his son.

When Ma turned a hundred in March 2017, she received this lovely letter from a lady called Mrs Sayanti Gupta in Calcutta, who remembered that her grandfather had been a correspondent on a Calcutta newspaper during Ma's visit.

At the outset please accept heartiest congratulations on your 100th birthday. I have been meaning to write in for a long time — as my grandfather had covered your visit to Calcutta in the early 1940s as a correspondent of a local newspaper. He also loved your movies — which he reviewed!

You have been a shining beacon of hope to his

generation as well as to all of us. Your songs will always be immortal and you remain one of our greatest inspirations in the present troubled times we inhabit.

Of course I am very proud to hear things like this about my mother, and I know that she touched not just British people, but people across the world. I also think it is important to remember that so many other nationalities were in the Fourteenth Army — and that they all made enormous sacrifices in order that the war against the Japanese was won.

My mother's sacrifice was small compared to many of those men, but as a young woman thousands of miles away from home in unfamiliar conditions, and with her most important asset — her voice — being strained to its limit, I am sure she must have been a little nervous that she would not be able to do what she had set out to do. Like anyone who is struggling with the thing that is most important for their livelihood — a writer with writer's block, or an athlete with an injury — she doubtless had some anxiety. Fortunately, she managed to get a few days of rest before heading on towards Burma, and I'm sure this helped her a great deal, especially given the fact that she was able to do some swimming. She has always loved swimming and still has a pool in her back garden now. This gave her the chance to rest her body and her voice as she began her journey towards the jungle and the front line of Burma.

Reaching the Forgotten Army

Vera

On Saturday morning, 22 April 1944, I got on the postal delivery plane from Calcutta's Dum Dum airport at 8.15 and we made two stops to deliver the mail before arriving in Chittagong, in what is now Bangladesh, but which was then on the furthest edge of eastern Bengal, at eleven in the morning. From here on in, ENSA, which was a civilian body, could no longer take responsibility for me as they considered the conditions to be too dangerous, and so I put myself in the hands of the army as I began the final journey to the front line.

In Chittagong I stayed at the Officers' Club, and the first thing I did when I got there was to have a bath in a tin tub. The club, I gathered, had originally been built to accommodate officials related to the tea industry, which was one of Bengal's biggest exports and was shipped out of the port of Chittagong in enormous quantities. I have always loved a good cup of tea, but I was yet to be convinced by the idea of drinking it in the heat of India. Whilst soaking in the bath in the club, I thought of how much it reminded me of the old hand-filled bath that we used to have when I lived in Ladysmith Avenue, East Ham. I think that growing up in that environment probably made me more resilient to

93

little hardships in life, and there in that bath I felt utterly happy to have found a little peace and solitude, in what was probably one of the more luxurious places in Chittagong, before launching into the next round of visits and shows.

After I had freshened up, I went and did a hospital visit, which involved a by-now-familiar tour of the boys in their hospital beds, with lots of chatting. I then did a show in the hospital canteen in a raucous atmosphere. The crowd was terrific; the note in my diary even says 'police needed', such was the clamour to hear me sing! It was much later, at Dimapur, that Jimmy Reed came to one of my concerts, but the atmosphere he described in a letter to me was much the same as on this evening.

I rolled up more than an hour before the show was due to commence in the hope that I could be allowed to do my little bit by escorting some major or captain to a front seat. I hadn't been in the theatre more than five minutes and the crowds ran over the place. Police in countless numbers, even brigadiers couldn't make the slightest impression on the crowd when the rightful owners came to collect their seat. Things were left to stand much to the disgust of many a fine officer.

The majority of the crowd present at that first show were, as you know, lads right out of the front line, fellows who had spent the last few months under the worst conditions imaginable, and due back at any moment to the same fate. Your appearance on the stage had the effect or command that every CO in the British Army would like to think or consider was his. A gesture to sing and all was quiet. Of course, I can't imagine any CO wanting to sing or even speak civilly to his underdogs, but that's how it struck me, and to sit out in front and watch the reactions made me wonder. A CO with your command over the same crowd of fellows would be a Godsend to any army.

Looking back on it now, the memories are not always distinct — they tend instead to merge together — so my diary is a very necessary part of remembering the events of so long ago.

As well as singing, the boys always wanted me to sign things for them, but there was so little paper around that it was sometimes difficult to find things to scribble on. The most popular solution was to sign one-rupee notes; but I did also end up signing all kinds of other things too: hats, for instance, and even cars and planes! My shows all tended to proceed along similar lines and I performed what I believed the boys wanted to hear, which was mainly my biggest hits, crowd-pleasers such as 'We'll Meet Again', 'White Cliffs of Dover', 'You'll Never Know', 'Roll Out the Barrel' and the love song 'Yours', which was always a particular favourite of the servicemen. In some ways I felt that I could sing anything and they would be happy, so I sometimes threw in a cover of someone else's song as well. One of these — 'If I Had My Way'

— was always greeted with laughter because, I suppose, there was an obvious innuendo and you have to remember that many of them had had little or no contact with women, sometimes for years! They were no doubt thinking of what they would do if they had *their* way, despite the fact that the song is written from the point of view of a woman. Looking back on it, I realise that I was naive, not just about things like that, but in many other ways.

The boys may have been thinking these things, but they were, without exception, decent and honourable to me. They were never what I would describe as rowdy. Mostly they sang along with me and enjoyed themselves. They always seemed

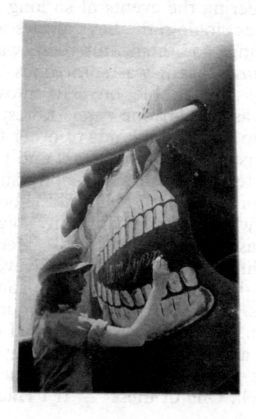

pleased to see me and in good spirits. They would shout out to me between the songs, asking questions and making requests — all in the friendliest spirit. I had the feeling that they just wanted to engage with me, to start a conversation, and possibly to say to their chums that they had spoken to me. There were some of them who were relatively new arrivals, but a lot of the troops had been in India and Burma since before the war and clearly felt completely cut off from what was happening at home.

Sometimes it was all too much, and there were tears — occasionally during the concerts and more often when I was alone with them, talking to them individually. It was quite clear that they saw me as a link with home and that aroused a lot of different emotions — joy at being reminded of that connection; and sorrow because they longed for home and it seemed so far away. Some of them said things to me along the lines of 'England doesn't feel that far away because you're here.' It was impossible for me to be impassive through all of this — I saw the happiness, hope and sadness move across their faces, and I felt those emotions too. As a singer, I always felt it was important to be in touch with how my audiences felt, and I think too that many of them were younger than me, which roused, if not a maternal instinct, then at least that of an elder sister.

That first Sunday on the road was 23 April, and throughout the tour, Sundays, which in those days still held significance as the one day in the week that was really quite distinct from all the others, became a day for mainly talking to the boys, wherever I was. That first Sunday we sat and drank tea and chatted very informally. I laughed when some of them said they could not believe I had flown out there just to entertain them! I don't think it was a grand gesture, but I was pleased to see that it meant so much. In the afternoon we drove to the coast along the most terrible road I had ever driven down and had afternoon tea and sandwiches overlooking the sea.

March and April are the hottest months in that part of the world, and it felt like it the following day: I had never been so hot in my life. That day, 24 April, I did a concert for about a thousand troops at the YMCA and afterwards signed hundreds of autographs. I was not used to singing in those kind of temperatures and I needed to have a wash and a change of clothes before I did my next concert, which happened to be a show for 600 officers. There weren't often separate shows for officers and other ranks and I'm not sure why it happened this time. It may have been here where Willie Smith saw me sing. He wrote to me to tell me:

For a short while we forgot the condition we were living under. The kind of food we had to eat, the water we had to drink. It was a still evening but clammy so that as well as wiping away the perspiration there were a few tears mixed in with it when we all joined in to sing your final song 'We'll Meet Again'.

This had seldom been a problem back home, but I found that more often than not when I was in Burma I would be so drenched with perspiration that my clothes would stick to me. Most often I performed in a khaki uniform; very occasionally I put on the one pink dress I had brought with me.

I did two further shows on 25 April for the RAF, and then the following day — a steaming-hot Wednesday — we set off south down the Arakan Road into the hottest and most humid part of Burma, towards places like Cox's Bazar, Maungdaw and Ramu airfield. It was to be a terrible journey down appallingly bumpy tracks. Our poor piano suffered almost as much as us — while we were there it fell out of tune all the time with the vibration from poor surfaces and the heat and humidity. After one journey, it seemed fine on the stage, but as soon as Len started playing it, the poor thing fell apart! Some of the boys climbed up onto the stage and held it together — successfully — while I sang! We travelled in two vehicles — Len and I were in the first vehicle with a driver and either an officer or an NCO, and then we had a small truck carrying the upright piano, our microphones and our rudimentary public address system. We usually ran this from the headlights of the vehicles when we travelled around — without it the boys would not have been able to hear me. Len wore an enormous Smith & Wesson revolver on his hip the entire time!

When I look back now at those shows at various units, to audiences ranging from a handful of men to a thousand, it felt like they followed each other in a bewildering succession. There was little to distinguish one event from another except that at one reinforcement camp I remember hearing the awful yelping of jackals for the first time and it felt like some kind of call from the wild, as though I was now leaving any semblance of civilisation and heading into a place where the laws I had been used to all my life had been replaced by something altogether more savage and unknown.

Ginny

Chittagong, situated very close to the border of Burma, and occupying a highly strategic position at the apex of the Bay of Bengal, was an important air, naval and military base for the Allied forces throughout the Burma campaign. It was also a key target for the Japanese, who hoped to capture it on the way to Calcutta as they swept north and westwards, up along the Arakan coast and into India. General Slim had found it both militarily vulnerable and rather gloomy when he first visited it in 1942:

> *My first impression of Chittagong, the only port of consequence on the whole coast and therefore of primary importance in any advance, was not reassuring. The Japanese had bombed it once or twice, not very seriously, but some partially trained non-regular Indian troops, who formed its garrison, had not stood even that light introduction to warfare well; there was a distinctly jumpy feel about the place.*

Elsewhere, he wrote:

> *Chittagong was a melancholy place. It had not been badly knocked about, but the light bombing it had suffered had driven out a large part of its inhabitants. Those who remained, the poorest,*

were menaced by approaching famine. The railway workshops, formerly the chief industry of the town, had been dismantled when it looked as if the Japanese would advance into Bengal, and even the roofs had been removed. The docks, whose demolition had been stopped just in time, were a brighter spot. Under the energetic drive of Hallet, the naval officer in charge, and of some devoted civilians, the quays were beginning to show great activity. In peace, Chittagong must have been the most attractive of the larger towns of Bengal; now, its general air of neglect, stagnation, and apprehension was depressing.

Captain Ian Wallace recalled in his memoirs:

The Chittagong reinforcement camp was not uncomfortable and the tents were pitched high up on sand dunes giving a magnificent view of the Chittagong jungles. My tent companion got dysentery badly but did not go to the hospital as he was just out from England and hardly wanted to retire immediately to bed. The sanitation was rudimentary though we fed comparatively well. Here I first saw a Japanese prisoner bowing and scraping to everyone in the most servile manner. Occasionally we were able to visit Chittagong though the bazaar there was hardly worthy of the name. There was a cinema but it was a good four miles from the town and not a tempting walk at midnight.

My mother visited Chittagong more than once while she was on her tour, and on one of those

102

occasions she toured a hospital. Flight Lieutenant W. A. Procter, a doctor at the hospital, wrote a letter home to his mother to tell her about the visit. She in turn wrote to Ma to ask if she remembered the incident

Recently I had a letter from my son — a Dr and F/Lt 61 Mobile Field Hospital Chittagong. He had shown you round the operating theatre and the anaesthetic apparatus and as you left — you left with 'a smile and a wave of the hand'.

I am his mother & I thank you — for it cheered him up so, a wave of the hand and a smile — like it was from someone — from the homeland — & it meant so much.

Do you remember the incident with F/Lt W. A. Procter (who incidentally is the son of a doctor killed in the last war — hence my name as I remarried ten years ago)?

If you do — & can spare the time — do please tell me how he was at the time. I should appreciate news of him from someone who has so recently seen him. He always says he is OK.

Corporal Horace Powell of the Royal Welsh Fusiliers was the batman/cook to General Piggott and had been in Burma since 1942. His brother Ronald was a sergeant in the same regiment. At one point in the conflict Horace's platoon was lost in the jungle and his family were notified that he was 'missing, presumed killed'. However, reports of his demise at this stage had been exaggerated — he walked out of the jungle and lived to fight another day. It also meant

103

that he was able to listen to Ma sing. His daughter wrote a letter to Ma in 2012 in which she said:

> Dad's favourite memory was when he and his brother heard you sing — you landed in Chittagong and then faced a 3 mile journey into the jungle to bring some much needed delight to 'the forgotten army'. Dad didn't have any writing paper — all he could find was a rupee note, which he tore in half and asked you to sign both parts. Dad kept one part and his brother kept the other. I wished I had still got this memento — but it got lost whilst Dad was serving in Japan and later Palestine.

Despite the happy memory of listening to my mother sing, the war was not kind to Horace Powell. His daughter writes that 'Dad's experiences in Burma led to him becoming mentally disturbed throughout his life — despite him being loved deeply by both my mother and I.'

The trauma of being a part of the Burma campaign deeply affected many of those who survived it, and it is a common theme of letters Ma received from children and grandchildren of servicemen that her visit was in many cases the *only* story that they told. Mrs Christine Cavanagh wrote to tell Ma about her father Gerry Wright:

> My father served in the 14th Army (the forgotten army) in Burma from 1943 to the end of the war. He would never talk about his time except for your visit which was such a morale boost for the troops. Being so far away there was no contact

with home, letters were very few and far between and were censored, your songs brought him closer to home & my mother to whom he was devoted. A very emotional man, any time he heard you it would bring him to tears. Your visit and what you did for him was something he appreciated and held you in high regard and affection for the rest of his life.

Similarly, Lorraine Jones, the daughter of Arthur Albert Jones, a mechanic in the RAF in Burma, wrote to say that her father 'spoke fondly of the people he met in the Far East. He was a great fan of yourself and thought that you were wonderful travelling to Burma and of course very brave. He also spoke about you entertaining the troops at that and could not praise you enough. However, he did not speak much about the war itself.' And a further example came from Marion Lane, whose father John Sampson served in the Manchester Regiment in Burma:

Dad would never speak about his time in Burma, apart from one thing, of which he spoke with great passion, and that was Vera Lynn coming out to entertain the troops. Dame Vera Lynn was my dad's hero.

You brought so much pleasure and light relief to the boys out there.

My dad was just so proud that Vera Lynn had signed his hat, that was such a proud moment for him; I just wish I knew what happened to that hat.

Signing autographs was a major task for Ma, and she signed all kinds of things, but rupee notes were definitely the most popular — I suppose that was the one piece of paper that most men dependably had in their pockets. Another recipient of one of these signed notes was Sergeant Major Jackson, whose daughter Patricia wrote in 2012 to say:

The one thing he was so proud of was that he carried you through the mud to the stage for your performance. He kept with him a signed rupee note for many years (now sadly lost) and until he passed away in 1979 spoke fondly of how you kept the spirits up for all of them in what must have been hell on earth, and they were not the forgotten army.

Requests for signed photographs were also a very common feature of the letters that Ma received during the war, including those that she was sent in Burma.

This was my mother's first foray into the jungle, and as well as the heat and humidity, the insects and much larger creatures, the jungle also seemed to possess a mystique that Slim and others were keen to dispel. Part of this was the sheer unfamiliarity of everything within the jungle to the average Tommy — harmless-looking leaves with minute hairs that would produce a poisonous sting, caterpillars that would leave a burning trail as they brushed against skin as soldiers moved through the undergrowth. The troops also had to adjust to the incredibly dense foliage, which meant that it was difficult to ever see further than a few metres at a time. To illustrate the degree to which this could happen, one veteran of the Burmese jungles wrote in the *Evening Standard* in 1944 that:

> *An elephant is an animal of great bulk, yet it is not uncommon to find oneself close enough to a wild elephant to hear it breathe, flap its ears and swish its tail — yet be unable to see an inch of the huge brute! If this is true of a beast standing eight feet high at the shoulder and weighing several tons, how much easier it is for the smaller animals to remain hidden.*

Similarly, he wrote about water sources that 'One can sometimes hear running water, but cannot see it through the dense foliage which can only be negotiated after a way has been cut.'

Imagine then the surprise of a young infantry officer

called Peter Saloman, who found a picture of Ma in the middle of the jungle.

I was leading a patrol through the dense jungle, laboriously cutting down the undergrowth as we went — it was incredibly hot and steamy and we were flagging a bit when we suddenly saw a glamorous picture of you, crudely framed and suspended from a tree — I believe it was a cut-out from the American forces' newspaper. The impact on all of us was absolute magic and had the instant effect of hugely raising our spirits! A lively discussion followed as to whether to take the picture with us and it was decided it should be left where it was — it is nice to think any following troops would benefit from the sight of it — we went on our way much heartened!

In his book *Burma '44*, historian James Holland tells the story of Trooper John Leyin, a young man who had joined the army and sailed to India on his first posting, where he joined the 25th Dragoons. After further training in India, he headed to the front, stopping along the way to see my mother singing just outside Chittagong. Holland writes:

Leyin was entranced. It was late afternoon, the sun was setting behind the trees, and the cacophony of insects and birds had died down, leaving the Forces Sweetheart the stage to herself. 'It was,' he wrote, 'far more than simply a concert. With her wonderful voice it was — and she made it so — our connection with home.'

While Ma was heading down the Burma Road in the last days of April, the fighting much further north at Kohima was at its bloodiest and most intense. The ridge at Kohima, a staging post between the strategic railhead at Dimapur (forty-six miles to the north) and the plain at Imphal (around eighty miles to the south), included an army barracks, a reinforcement camp and an Indian general hospital. The ridge was at 5,000 feet and the Dimapur-Imphal road ran along it for a few miles. The Deputy Commissioner's bungalow, the adjacent tennis court, and Garrison Hill above them, somewhere around the middle of this ridge, became an apocalyptic battleground for over a month, as Japanese and Allied forces fought for control of the high ground. If the Japanese had control, it meant that they could limit supplies and reinforcements going down to the battle at Imphal and press on into India. As in the Battle of the Admin Box, though, the Allied forces at Kohima when the attack arrived were not the strongest — and they were facing a Japanese force that was far larger than Slim had initially anticipated.

The total number of Allied troops in and around Kohima at the start of April was only around 3,000, and this force comprised a diverse mixture of fighting ability and experience. It included the Assam Regiment, the Assam Rifles, the local police force, an inexperienced battalion — the Shere Regiment — of the Nepalese army and a battalion of the Burma Regiment. There were also some Indian regiments, the Indian Army Service Corps and around 500 patients who were convalescing in the relatively cool climate high up in the hills. Their convalescence was destined to be short-lived: these men were issued with arms, organised into units and sent to man the defences.

Those who were deemed too ill to fight were evacuated, along with all other non-combatants; further trenches were dug and dressing stations were prepared.

When the scale of the attack became clear, reinforcements were called in, but by the time the Japanese 31st Division had cut off the road, only one battalion — the 4th Battalion of the Queen's Own Royal West Kent Regiment (the 'West Kents') — had made it through. Slim feared that the Japanese would cut straight through to Dimapur, and so defences were also prepared there as well. Major Harry Smith was the officer commanding HQ Company in the Queen's Own Royal West Kent Regiment. He remembers:

We left the meagre garrison at Kohima and various odd bodies from the convalescent depot. No sooner were we back at Dimapur, than orders came through for the brigade to move up [to Kohima] once more, but by this time the leading Japanese spearheads were on the outskirts of Kohima. As we wound up the road again, we met crowds of frightened non-combatants. The battalion was leading the brigade column and as it approached Kohima it came under heavy fire from machine guns and artillery.

The day that Ma arrived in Calcutta, on 6 April 1944, was also the day that the siege of Kohima began. The Japanese had been attacking the ridge since the afternoon of the 3rd, and the position had been gradually deteriorating since that time, to the extent that by the 6th, the defenders found themselves overrun by enemy forces. General Slim recalled in his book:

Early on the morning of the 6th, a company of Rajputs [Indian soldiers] got into Kohima and one platoon of it brought out two hundred walking wounded and non-combatants. During the morning, however, the Japanese closed round the town, and the [161] Brigade was unable to gain the ridge. The road behind was soon afterwards cut by a strong enemy detachment who established a block between the brigade and Dimapur. The situation at Kohima was thus: its garrison of about three thousand men closely invested by superior forces, 161 Brigade cut off five miles to the north [. . .] and the base itself in no state to resist a serious attack.

As my mother struggled with her voice in Calcutta, the soldiers in Kohima faced a much more serious challenge. When the Japanese advanced onto the ridge on 6 April, they also gained possession of the water supply, and the area held by Allied soldiers was reduced from a square of approximately 1,000 yards to one of 500. Harry Smith recalled: 'We very soon ran out of water when the Japanese cut the only piped supply. Luckily a spring was discovered near my company area, and hazardous trips had to be organised every night.'

The Japanese launched wave after wave of attacks, sacrificing many men in the process, but slowly shrinking the Allied perimeter, until by 9 April most of the action was concentrated around the tennis court next to the Deputy Commissioner's bungalow. Major John Winstanley of the West Kents told how 'we held the tennis court against desperate attacks for five days'.

The conditions became truly horrendous as more bodies from both sides fell on the battlefield. Harry Smith describes how 'The smell of death increased as the days passed and bodies decomposed. Day after day our hopes were dashed when expected relief did not arrive. We began to walk about like zombies because we had little chance of sleep.'

There are many stories of incredible courage on the ridge over those days of intense fighting. One of the most remarkable is that of Lance Corporal John Harman, who on two separate occasions took on enemy positions by himself. On the first occasion he threw a grenade into a Japanese machine-gun bunker, then entered the bunker, killing both the occupants and emerging with the gun. The following day, on 9 April, he asked his mates to give him covering fire as he ran down a hill to stop Japanese soldiers digging in to new positions. When he tried to return to his own lines, he was caught in the back by machine-gun fire and fell to the floor. His commanding officer, Captain Donald Easten, risked his own life to crawl forward and drag him back to safety, but when he got to him, Harman said: 'Don't bother, sir . . . I got the lot. It was worth it.' Those were Harman's final words as he died in Easten's arms. Harman was later posthumously awarded the Victoria Cross. The official citation stated that: 'Lance-Corporal Harman's heroic action and supreme devotion to duty were a wonderful inspiration to all and were largely responsible for the decisive way in which all attacks were driven off by his Company.'

The West Kents had to wait until the night of 19 April for relief to arrive, but the new troops coming up to the ridge had also had to fight their way through before engaging with the enemy entrenched at Kohima. Major Harry Smith, who had been there since the beginning of the siege, was about to head to the battalion HQ to receive orders for the relief when a mortar bomb burst on the front of the trench he was in and a piece of shrapnel hit him in the face, knocking him out. He was given a shot of morphine and woke the following morning to see the leading troops of the Royal Berkshire Regiment coming up the hill in 'their nice clean uniforms'. The contrast with the filthy, exhausted troops of the West Kents could not have been greater. Smith remembers:

Soon I was being helped down the hill to the waiting ambulances, together with the remnants of the battalion, who were filing down ragged, bearded, looking like scarecrows. Tanks were engaging enemy positions on the road. I never thought we would be overwhelmed as the Japs were taking enormous casualties. I was taken to the hospital at Dimapur and had a restless night listening to the cries of the wounded.

The first part of the Battle of Kohima was over. The initial defenders had managed to hold on to the centre of the ridge, and General Slim paid tribute to those soldiers who had stood firm. 'Sieges have been longer but few have been more intense, and in none have the defenders deserved greater honour than the garrison of Kohima.'

However, the situation was still extremely dangerous and most of the ridge remained in enemy hands. The Japanese were deeply dug in on a succession of steep wooded slopes and the flanks of their position extended out into high, inaccessible jungle surrounding the ridge. Slim remarked that it was 'as formidable a position as a British army has ever faced'. Having successfully broken the siege, the task faced by the Fourteenth Army now was to dislodge the enemy from this position. While my mother toured through Burma, from Chittagong down the coast in the Arakan to Maungdaw, from Feni to Comilla and Dimapur, this was what was taking place in Kohima.

Major Francis Boshell of the Royal Berkshire Regiment was in Kohima for three weeks, and his men were attacked every single night.

They came in waves, like a pigeon shoot. Most nights they overran part of the battalion position, so we had to mount counter-attacks. When part of my right-hand platoon was overrun, we winkled them out with the bayonet. I lost two platoon commanders, but good sergeants took over, and did better. Water was short and restricted to about one pint per man per day, so we stopped shaving. Air supply was the key, but the steep terrain and narrow ridges meant that some of the drops went to the enemy. My company went into Kohima over one hundred strong and came out at about sixty.

The fighting was so extreme that General John Grover, a divisional commander who had fought in the First World War, said that it was worse than battles he had been at in the Somme — one of the most horrendous conflicts in human history. I think this kind of detail is important in trying to understand what my mother's visit meant to troops who had been involved in the fighting. In a trench on a hillside in Kohima, in the dark, in the quiet moments between attacks, there must have been some desperate moments of intense loneliness, isolation and fear that I cannot even imagine. For those soldiers who were able to get away from the front line and hear my mother sing, most probably at Dimapur, the opportunity to feel some kind of connection with home and hear the warmth of her voice must have been truly amazing.

A few years ago, an author and ex-RAF pilot called Roger Annett asked my mother to write a preface for his book about the RAF's contribution in Burma, called *Drop Zone Burma*. He writes about how Ma 'was tireless in her efforts to entertain the boys brought down the road from Kohima and flown in from Imphal to be patched up, operated on, and too often, to die, in the base hospitals of Dimapur. She sat at the foot of beds in the tented wards, smiled, signed autographs, got the occasional kiss — and sang her songs.' There was no doubt, as some of the letters the men wrote to her admitted, that she sometimes inspired homesickness, but more often, as Annett writes, 'What she brought was a reminder of their wives and sweethearts at home and a reassurance that they weren't forgotten. She had come all the way out there to see them — and they loved her.'

Ann James, the daughter of General Sir Philip Christison, who commanded XV India Corps during the Burma campaign, wrote that her father used to tell the story of how, when he introduced Vera at one of her concerts, he also gave her a big kiss. He then said: 'I have kissed Vera Lynn more times than my wife in this war!' I don't think there were too many kisses; if anything, I get the impression that lots of the boys were overly reserved when they actually met my mother. Many of them had been abroad for months and even years with very little female company. One collectively written letter, for instance, was at pains to make my mother feel as though her visit had been a success, because they were clearly worried that they had not been expressive enough. 'We can assure you that all the lads appreciate your splendid efforts, even if some of us are too 'tongue-tied' to say so,' they wrote.

Although my mother was most often the only Western woman of any kind at the various bases and camps she visited, there were also a handful of women called the Women's Auxiliary Service Burma (known as the 'Wasbies'), who manned mobile canteens for the servicemen, selling cups of tea and pieces of cake as well as cigarettes, soap and razor blades. They wore jungle-green uniform dresses and berets or head-scarves during the day, and shirts and trousers in the evening to protect their legs from mosquito bites. On their way up from Imphal in March, at the start of the offensive, a group of them had almost been cut off by the Japanese: fourteen Wasbies in two mobile canteens, as well as a group of nurses in ambulances, narrowly escaped a roadblock. Joan Morton was one of them; she remembered going up into the hills to Kohima from Dimapur after the fighting in June 1944 and described what an apocalyptic sight it was.

Kohima was high up in the mountains above Dimapur and for weeks we had heard the sound of unceasing gunfire, but it was my first experience of seeing a battlefield at close quarters

116

— burnt tree stumps, deserted trenches and dugouts, pervaded by the sickly smell of Japanese dead bodies. It was a sight I was to become accustomed to over the next twelve months.

Slim was confident after the initial defence of the ridge that his army would be victorious — not just at Kohima, but also at Imphal to the south as well. Whereas the conflict at Kohima involved the defence of a single strategic position, the battle at Imphal was much more geographically and operationally complex. The town of Imphal stood on a plain approximately forty miles long and twenty miles wide. The plain had become an important operational centre for the Fourteenth Army, and in particular for Lieutenant General Scoones's IV Corps. It contained a number of airfields, hospitals and supply dumps, while the town of Imphal itself was at the centre of three main strategic roads — one to Kohima and Dimapur (to the north), one to Tiddim (due south), and one to Sittaung (south-east).

The opening phase of the Battle of Imphal took place at the start of March as the Japanese 33rd Division moved across the Chindwin River. Slim's strategy was for the most forward Allied divisions, principally the 17th, to fall back onto the plain and let the Japanese come on to them. However, Slim and Scoones miscalculated the timing of the Japanese offensive, and the enemy troops were able to get in behind the 17th Division, cutting them off from their intended retreat and threatening the town of Imphal itself with inundation. The Japanese made a concerted effort to take Imphal from the east, pushing forward first to Ukhrul and then to Sangshak. Here there was

117

fierce fighting from 21 to 26 March, before the Allied forces fell all the way back to Imphal. However, the damage inflicted on the advancing Japanese force was considerable, and slowed their momentum.

Meanwhile, the 23rd Indian Infantry Division had gone to the rescue of the 17th, and together they cleared the Japanese roadblock and pulled back to Imphal on 5 April. Much of the fighting that took place in the weeks following this withdrawal was for control of the roads, and there was a series of hard-fought battles in various places across the plain and in the surrounding hills. Much of the fighting was fierce and produced high numbers of casualties on both sides, such as at the battle for the Shenam Saddle and Palel Airfield. Corporal Stanley May was a stretcher-bearer in the Devonshire Regiment at Shenam Saddle at the start of April. His battalion was trying to take a hill at right angles to the saddle, but the Japanese troops were in strong defensive positions in deep bunkers. The Devonshires' commanding officer put up barbed wire around the hill, and that night the Japanese tried to counterattack through it. In the morning, May noticed that there were forty or so Japanese soldiers hanging on the wire. In their effort to take the hill, thirty-one men from 1st Battalion, Devonshire Regiment, were also killed.

As at Kohima, though, the Japanese attacking threat had mainly faded by the end of April, and Slim and Scoones began to plot the offensive that would turn the enemy around. Slim's confidence was well founded, as the Japanese had lost many more men than the Allied forces and had insufficient supplies for a long campaign. At the end of April, though, as my mother headed down towards the southernmost part of British-held Burma, there were many more weeks of hard fighting to be done, and the monsoon rains were on their way, which made the jungle an even more treacherous and forbidding place to be.

Singing for the Burma Boys

Vera

We headed south into the steamy heat along the Arakan Road on 26 April. The Arakan Road was the name given to the rough highway that headed south from Chittagong, first to the railhead at Dohazari then south along the flat coastal plains towards Maungdaw. The first concert I did on my journey south was at a hospital for the 81st (West African) Division on 26 April. They struck me, even in their beds, and convalescing in the hospital grounds, as a very smart and disciplined bunch of lads. Their divisional sign was a black spider against a yellow background, and most of the soldiers were from Nigeria, the Gold Coast, Sierra Leone and the Gambia, though there were also quite a few British boys there as well. In my diary I wrote that the African boys called me their 'white mumma', and some nice photos survive of my visit. I was pleased that it wasn't just the British boys who could appreciate my being there — I also sang for all the other men who made up the Fourteenth Army: the Gurkhas, the Indians and the Karen tribespeople among others.

After the hospital performance, we then did a show for between three and four thousand of the lads at Dohazari rest camp. Dohazari was at the railhead that ran from Chittagong thirty miles to the north and so was a place where supplies came in to and wounded men and soldiers heading out on leave would go out from. When I arrived at a place, I usually didn't know how many people I would be performing for, and I soon stopped being surprised by the numbers. At the most it was about 6,000. The smallest audience I had was just two. Regardless of the number of people in the audience, I can put my hand on my heart and say that I always tried to produce the best performance I possibly could. On the couple of occasions I sang for just two men, it was in a hospital and they were men who could not move from their beds. It is possible that I may have tried a little harder for them, as I could see how much it meant. Sometimes I would arrive at a place and it seemed as if almost nobody was there, but then the boys would magically emerge out of the tall grasses around a clearing; we would talk for a while, I would sign autographs for them and then I would sing for them.

The following day, 27 April, we continued south from Dohazari on the road towards the front line. Somewhere along this terrible bumpy track we were met by General Slim's car, which accompanied us to Bawli Bazar, over many of the tidal creeks known in Burma as *chaungs*. The weather was hot and sticky, and the air smelled of the sea and salt marshes. Somewhere along the way it seems that I passed by a man named John P. McCormack, who wrote to me afterwards.

I didn't have the good fortune to attend one of your shows in the many you gave to us in Burma, the nearest I got to you was when our convoy was held up on the Maungdaw Road, I saw you pass there. It was only a little incident in the life of our unit there, but I can assure you that every one of the boys in the unit are grateful to you for all those shows you did for our benefit, and we won't forget how you put up with all the hard going and discomfort when you could have stayed at home like so many of the other artistes have done, despite the need for more entertainment here. I've left Burma behind now and I will try to forget the hardships we went through, but I shall, like many of my comrades, always look back and admire your courage and unselfishness during this war.

The journey, which is recorded in my diary, took from half past eight in the morning until five in the afternoon, and at some point along the way we did another two shows, one of them at a dressing station, for the front was by that point not far away at all — probably no more than five miles, in fact. I remember this concert well, as the boys had arranged a little hut for me to get ready in. It even had its own dressing table, on which there stood a jam jar containing a small bunch of freshly picked jungle flowers. I thought that was such a wonderful gesture.

Bawli Bazar was a small place just off the Naf River, not far north of Maungdaw. It served as a base for troops fighting further inland in the densely forested hills of the Arakan. Joseph Green got in touch with me a few years ago to tell me that he remembered being at one of the performances I gave when I was in that part of Burma.

I am very pleased to say I was at your concert in a place called Bawli Bazar, & it was excellent, it was a grand link with home. I was a gunner with 1st Medium Regiment, Royal Artillery, in action about 4 miles away, with large 5.5 inch guns, 100lb shells, I was with 33 Corps SEAC Command as it was called in those days, my number was 942566, what days, we also had Cheryl Lind and Stainless Stephen to entertain us, you were soaked to death with sweat that day, I will never forget it.

It may also have been here at Bawli Bazar that Jack Pottrell, who wrote a letter to me after I had returned to England, heard me sing.

I don't suppose you will remember me, but when I was in the Royal Artillery, I once had my photograph taken with you, at a gun-site where you stopped on your way back from the Arakan front. I am very proud of that photo.

I wonder if you would sing a song for me sometime? I would like you to sing 'You'll Never Know' for the girl I hope to marry some day. Just say it's for 'Kay', she'll understand.

Of course, I could not possibly remember every single person that I met, especially as I spoke to thousands and thousands of servicemen when I was in Burma, but when I got home I did try to meet any requests that the boys made to me, either in person or by letter. Usually that meant playing or, as in this instance, singing songs on the radio and dedicating them to a wife or sweetheart, but there were sometimes other requests, such as the boy who asked me to lay some flowers on his mother's grave. His name was Ernest Preston, a trooper in the Reconnaissance Corps. His poor mum had sadly passed away while he was out in Burma and he asked if I could choose some flowers and take them to the cemetery. I felt so sorry for him and I was very pleased to be able to do something to help him. In fact, it was one of the very first things I did when I got home to England. I still have the note he sent to thank me:

May I take this opportunity of thanking you very sincerely for the great kindness you have been able to perform on my behalf. I have heard from home of your visit, and of the choice of flowers which I understand you had taken.

This was the only way possible for me to be able to pay my last respects to a devoted mother, and you have done something which no other person could so well for me.

I realise your visit has done much to strengthen the morale of those at home, in much the same manner as did the effect of

127

your tour in India have on our troops — we shall remember you with great admiration for your courage and devotion for the troops in India — I know because the boys are always speaking of you, in fact you are known as the 'Sweetheart of the 14th'.

However, it is really hard to find words to express my personal thanks and apprecia-tion, but this I am certain, you did it with all sincerity. May God bless & protect you and yours, and best wishes to you in your future career.

I was exhausted that night after travelling all day, and immediately after the show, I went straight to bed and fell asleep. The following day, 28 April, we visited a hospital where I spoke to lots of the boys, visiting them by their bedsides. I also had the chance to see the operating theatre that had been set up in a large tent. When I was there, an Indian soldier was having a bullet removed from his arm so I did not want to get in the way — and was also not particularly keen on standing by as a surgeon dug into someone's arm with a sharp knife — so I squeezed out of the tent. No sooner had I slipped out than the the surgeon called me back in asking, 'Would you like this for a souvenir?' He handed me the Japanese bullet that he had just taken out of the man's arm, wrapped in a piece of gauze and still bloody. I was rather shocked, but I kept this gory souvenir for many years. Sadly, it got lost when I loaned it to an exhibition a few years ago.

That kind of thing felt normal in the jungle,

however strange and macabre it may seem now. I was close to the war. I knew exactly where the boys were and what they were doing — they were fighting a terrible war. I wasn't afraid, though, because I knew they would look after me. But it wasn't easy. It was hot, always so hot. The bathroom facilities were never overly luxurious. I usually stayed in one of the bamboo huts — or *bashars* — in which there were generally two buckets. One had fresh water for washing; the other was your toilet. It paid to remember which was which! I had no problem with the arrangements; and although I didn't actively want to be deprived of the trappings of civilisation, I suppose there was a certain part of me that was keen to understand how the soldiers lived out there. Signing up for Burma meant really experiencing what our boys were going through — I knew that it would be basic, and that didn't bother me at all. That is, except for the insects, and I'll come to those in a bit.

Since I had my bath in Chittagong, it would be a few weeks before I could do so properly again, though the next day, on 29 April, I was at least able to go for a swim. After I was given the bullet (literally rather than figuratively!), I went to another hospital right on the front, and then off on a road that snaked through the jungle to the mouth of what I suppose must have been the Naf River. From the beach at Teknaf, we took a boat out to St Martin's Island, which I am reliably informed is Burma's only coral island, where I had a wonderfully refreshing swim. There I came across a group of RAF men on leave who were swimming in the sea when I arrived by boat. When they came out of the sea, I remarked on how strange it was that they should all be wearing white shorts. In fact it turned out they were not wearing white shorts at all, but because they had been wearing their khaki shorts for so long, the tan marks were especially pronounced. I still have some photographs that were taken out there — it was a beautiful place and felt about as far away from the war as you could possibly be. We stayed the night on the peninsula back on the mainland, and the following morning I was able to swim again before we travelled onwards.

Later that morning, we headed north again and did a show for 5,000 of the boys at Ramu airbase on the Baghkali River, just inland from Cox's Bazar, home of the world's longest beach. We were technically back in India, but it was still not that far away from the fighting, which just goes to show how close the Japanese got to coming over the border.

That night I had a particularly uncomfortable sleep as I lay precariously on a stretcher balanced between two kitchen chairs in a shed, struggling to keep myself enclosed within the mosquito net. In its own way it was an amusing episode, even at the time, but in the morning I was most certainly glad to leave.

The following day we went back to Chittagong and had lunch in a *bashar* before going to a hospital and doing a show at an ack-ack site. It was incredibly hot and humid; in my diary I simply wrote: 'Dinner, film, then bed — very sticky.' There followed some zigzagging around the place. From Chittagong we went to a place called Feni, right on the Burmese border, where I sang at a small mess in the very depths of the jungle. Somehow my bags had not arrived with me and so I had with me no alternative outfit, but the major very kindly let me borrow some clothes. I think in some of the photos you can see me wearing a pair of slacks that look far too big for me. I can honestly say that it is the only time I have ever performed while wearing men's trousers. The nights were uncomfortably hot there and I struggled to sleep in spite of my terrible tiredness. I found the time to write a few letters on the morning of 2 May — to Harry and my family, I expect — before doing two shows. I had an early night and tried to sleep in the heat.

On 3 May, we headed two hours up the road from Feni to the Fourteenth Army headquarters in Comilla, where we were to base ourselves for most of the following week. When General Slim took over the leadership of the army, he moved the headquarters there from Barrackpore, using an old college building, which, although it had been smartened up, still had a rather brooding air of sadness and neglect about it, with great patches of mildew on the walls from the humidity and the monsoons. One of the first people I met there was Major General Arthur Snelling — Slim's head of administration and a big cog in the complicated machine that was the Fourteenth Army. I noticed that it was not quite as hot as it had been down on the coast as the temperature felt much more comfortable;

nonetheless, the days that followed in the build-up to the monsoon were known to be the most uncomfortable of the year, and I must admit that I struggled with the humidity as much as the heat. I did two shows in Comilla town hall — a neat, symmetrical two-storey whitewashed building with a long veranda at the front and palm trees all around it.

The following day, I went to talk to the Chindits — the special forces who had just returned from behind enemy lines and who had to be deloused before I saw them! I did not sing for them; we just sat and chatted and I signed some autographs. I was really pleased to see them. They were curious about how people were coping at home. They said to me: 'When you get home, tell them about us; tell them to keep sending cigarettes through.' Arthur Baker, who wrote to me in 2012, remembered our meeting:

I had great pleasure of meeting you at the hospital in Comilla, we had just flown out from behind enemy lines in Burma. I was with the Chindits 16 Brigade, 2nd Battalion the Leicestershire Regt.

I believe you were visiting Comilla to give a concert for the RAF and kindly visited us at the hospital. It was in early May 1944 when you were sitting on the hospital bed talking and signing anything from bush hats to Japanese paper money. 68 years ago to the month that you visited us and I can still visualise you talking and laughing with us. The boost to our morale was terrific. From *being in the forgotten army to be known about by the forces' sweetheart was incredible and is a lasting memory to me, and it is part of my life story which I have written for my grandchildren.*

We spent over three months behind enemy lines so can you imagine our feeling to be meeting you within four or five days of landing at Comilla? I also had the pleasure of meeting you at the Bloomsbury Centre Hotel when you joined the Chindits and Admiral of the Fleet the Earl of Mountbatten of Burma, our patron for dinner.

No photographs I'm afraid, just memories, happy ones of meeting you.

Forgive the typing, arthritis in fingers making writing very difficult.

God bless you . . .

Arthur Baker

As Mr Baker mentions, I did a similar thing with some RAF boys later on that morning, as well as having my picture taken with them. And in the afternoon I had my picture taken with General Slim, who also came to see me sing that evening along with Air Commander Baldwin, who was the commander of the relatively new 3rd Tactical Air Force, which combined the US 5320th Air Defense Wing with the RAF's 221 and 224 Groups. This tactical air force also included an army support contingent that was essential in order to link together and supply all the different airfields in the region. Sadly, I do not know what happened to the photographs that were taken that day, but I have certainly never seen a copy of them. Many things got lost in the war, especially on the way back from Burma, so I assume this is what happened to those photographs. I remember that for the performance, I suppose because I thought it was a special one at the HQ, I wore my pink chiffon dress, which got darker and darker as I got hotter and hotter as I sang. I later joked that this dress, which had cost me a year's worth of coupons, was actually made out of two colours — pink and black!

General Slim was a great man and the boys loved him — he really was a soldier's soldier. It's nice when you have a man that the boys look up to so much; they felt the same about Mountbatten too. Because Comilla was the HQ, I met a lot of the senior ranks there, which I was quite used to by that time. They were all very kind to me, and Slim and Snelling in particular went out of their way to make sure that I had everything I needed.

Snelling wrote to me soon after with a kind note of thanks.

Dear Miss Lynn,
I am writing on behalf of the Army Commander to convey to you the sincere appreciation of all ranks of the Fourteenth Army for the splendid work which you did on your recent tour in the Army area. I need not tell you how much your efforts were appreciated — you are already aware of this I am sure — but I have received so many

*excellent reports of your visits to formations
and units that I feel I would like to put on
record this message of gratitude. It must
indeed be very gratifying to you to know
that you have been able to cheer front line
troops and sustain their high morale.*

*I hope we shall see you again, if there is
time for another visit before we have
defeated the Jap.*

All good wishes for a safe journey home.

Yours sincerely

Major General A. H. J. Snelling

As the heat built before the monsoon rains
came, I was getting more and more tired each
day. I did two more shows in Comilla on 5 May,
and had lunch in the junior ranks mess, while
on the 6th, I did a hospital visit and sang for
a crowd of three to four thousand. On the 8th,
I toured two hospitals, had dinner in the
sergeants' mess and did an open-air show for
3,000 troops. I recorded in my diary a couple of
times that I was tired; sometimes, as on 9 May,
when I had spent much of the day touring
hospitals before doing two shows in the evening,
I was 'dead tired'.

On 10 May, I flew in a Dakota from Comilla
to the remote RAF base at Agartala. One
interesting detail I noticed was that the RAF
roundel — the circular emblem that was on all
RAF aircraft — had a blue centre rather than a
red one in Burma. This was done in order to
distinguish the RAF aircraft from the Japanese
Zeros, which sported circular red emblems, like

D.O. No. 2418/9/A.

H.Q. Fourteenth Army,
12 A.B.P.O.
26 May 44.

Dear *Miss Lynn*,

     I am writing on behalf of the Army Commander to convey to you the sincere appreciation of all ranks of the Fourteenth Army for the splendid work which you did on your recent tour in the Army area. I need not tell you how much your efforts were appreciated - you are already aware of this I am sure - but I have received so many excellent reports of your visits to formations and units that I feel I would like to put on record this message of gratitude. It must indeed be very gratifying to you to know that you have been able to cheer front line troops and sustain their high morale.

     I hope we shall see you again, if there is time for another visit before we have defeated the Jap.

     All good wishes for a safe journey Home.

Yours *sincerely*

Maj-Gen A.H.J. Snelling.

Miss Vera Lynn,
c/o Ensa Area Officer,
Hong Kong House,
Council House Street,
CALCUTTA.

RAF aircraft in Europe. After having my photo taken with some of the RAF boys, I did a show in the dirt-floored *bashar* that was used as the mess and had lunch with the boys. This was also the same sort of hut that I would often be accommodated in for the night. When I woke up in the morning, I would wash using the bucket of fresh water that was provided for me, then, rather than pouring the water down the sink, or a drain, I would let it soak away into the floor.

That night, I did a further show at the cinema at Agartala and had dinner with 191 Squadron, who flew reconnaissance and meteorological flights in a type of aircraft called the Catalina. A man called Harry Procter sent me a very kind note about my performance that night, in which he wrote:

> First of all I want to thank you from the bottom of my heart, for the splendid performance you gave us all tonight. We gave you a great reception at the cinema, but I feel that in itself does not show our full appreciation for what you have done. If you could oblige me with an autographed photograph, I will cherish it and keep it always. You earned the title of 'Sweetheart of the Forces', way back in Blighty, somebody ought to get cracking now with, I suggest, 'Sweetheart of the Jungle'. You are the first English girl I have seen or heard in this part of the world. To my way of thinking, in taking on this arduous work you rank with Joan of Arc. May God bless & protect you safely back to England.

While I was in Agartala, I received this lovely note from Brigadier Henry back in Chittagong, thanking me on behalf of all the men down there for my efforts:

> On your departure from 404 area may I on behalf of all ranks of all services in my area thank you for your refreshing interlude in our daily duties. Your visit was deeply appreciated especially by those in hospital and you have brought to all a breath of ENGLAND and the homes we love. May the rest of your tour be a huge success. We wish you the very best of luck and a safe journey. To the above I would add my own personal thanks and good wishes.

Another document has survived that records something of these few days — a programme that was drawn up for me, with military precision, detailing where I should be and what I should be doing for virtually every minute of each day! On 11 May I went to the hospital in the morning to do a show out in the open where there was a large crowd. My diary records that I christened a jeep, which must have been at 216 Squadron, then soon after had lunch there at the regular (rather than the officer's) mess. I then went on to 31 Squadron for dinner before doing two shows at the cinema in the evening — the first at 2030 hours; the second at 2145 hours. Then I remember going back to the hospital (called the 'station sick quarters' on my itinerary) for drinks before collapsing into bed in a state of near exhaustion. Memories of those days in and around Agartala and Comilla tend to merge into one, but a couple of things certainly stand out. I remember improvising a stage made out of aircraft engine crates (some with the engines still in them), and being presented with a beautiful bunch of flowers that had been picked from the jungle, and which were wrapped in surgical gauze — one of the few materials of which there was plenty. The photograph of me holding these flowers with a large group of boys around me remains one of my favourite pictures of my time in Burma. When we put a piece in the newspapers just a few years ago, I was amazed at how many people came forward to say that their relatives were in that photograph. They included Cliff Hern, who circled his father, Victor Hern of the Royal Signals, in the picture and told an amusing story about him: 'My father loved telling the story about how you passed him and his colleagues whilst they were bathing naked in a river. I'm glad that the men were wearing clothes in the picture!'

Mary Sharples also got in touch to say that her father, Joseph Julier, who was with the RAF ground crew, was in the photograph. She wrote that she went to see him off as he sailed east when she was just four years old; she was seven when he came home and he felt like a stranger to her. She mentions that, like many of the men, he never spoke to her of his experiences in the war.

Mrs V. J. Howard was another who both recognised her father, Frederick Chapman, in that same photograph, and who said that he never really spoke to her about the war.

I cannot tell you a lot about when he was in Burma but I know a little bit of what he told me, he didn't like to talk about what he had been through.

I saw this group picture of you and your boys in the newspaper and straight away saw my father in the picture — I have put a ring around him. I don't know where it was taken or indeed that he had met you.

He told me that he was in Singapore and he had to swim across a river to get away from the Japs, he made it across but his friend didn't, he drowned. My father tried to save him but couldn't, he just about made it himself.

The next day we flew on — for more shows, more adventures and more heat. But the weather was breaking; monsoon season was now upon us, and heavy rain was on its way of the kind I had only seen in London once or twice in my life.

Ginny

One of the remarkable things about the front line in Burma was that it effectively extended for the many hundreds of miles that then made up the Indo-Burmese border — from the Bay of Bengal to the foothills of the Himalayas, from Maungdaw in the south to Ledo in the north, covering coastal plains, rice paddies, jungles and mountains. For the generals, that meant all kinds of logistical nightmares about how to conduct warfare; for my mother, it meant an awful lot of travelling down jungle tracks and over bumpy roads, on planes and boats, to make sure that as many troops as possible along this line were able to see her performing.

The journey south to Bawli Bazar took Ma close to the site of the Fourteenth Army's first significant military success, the Battle of the Admin Box, back in February. Where she sang would have been within earshot of the Japanese troops, just four miles away according to one soldier's letter. If they did hear her sing, I wonder what they thought. Just imagine her voice, which has always been so distinctive and resonant, and able to be projected long distances, swirling around through those forested hillsides. Perhaps a group of Japanese soldiers dug into a bunker looked at one another in bafflement and amazement at the sound emanating from the valley below. Perhaps it made them think of sweethearts they had left at home.

Flying Officer Lesley George Whitworth was a twenty-five-year-old reconnaissance pilot in 1944, and while off duty he was given the task of driving my mother around to some of the various sites in the Arakan. He also wrote occasional press releases and articles. Shortly after her appearance at Cox's Bazar, he penned this piece, with the headline: 'FRONT LINE SWEETHEART: In an interview with Vera Lynn'.

And it is no misnomer when the sweetheart in question goes up close enough to the firing lines to hear the bangs. That is precisely Vera Lynn's idea of a tour of entertainment.

After all,' she reasons, 'I'm supposed to be entertaining the forces. A lot of them can't come to me, so I have just got to go to them.'

Vera, at present touring the length and breadth of the forward areas of Bengal, has just moved

Len Edwards. Vera Lynn.

FRONT LINE SWEETHEART.   F/O L.G. WHITWORTH

In an interview with Vera Lynn.

And it is no misnomer when the sweetheart in question
goes up close enough to the firing lines to hear the bangs.
That is precisely Vera Lynn's idea of a tour of entertainment.

"After all," she reasons, "I'm supposed to be entertaining
the forces.   A lot of them can't come to me, so I have just
got to go to them."

Vera, at present touring the length and breadth of the
forward areas of Bengal, has just moved back slightly from a
spot very, very close to the action zone - so close, in fact,
that Len Edwards, manager and celebrated accompanist, was
wishing that he had brought along a good, loud grand piano to
drown the bangs, instead of the tiny, gentle, pianissimo job
he is carrying around in his waistcoat pocket.

But Vera - bless her golden tonsils - so tired in the
midst of so strenuous a tour, had to be awakened so that she
could listen.

She is going forward again in a couple of days but, of
course, her exact destinations must be confidential, if not
a military secret; from a morale standpoint she is the best
little thing that ever happened out here.   If you doubt it
listen to the applause.

Vera still has a lot of performances before she considers
her tour complete, and she will have to crowd them into a very
short space of time for she is returning to England in a few
weeks to keep a date with a picture at Columbia Studios.

"And thanks a lot for everything," she says, "I've enjoyed
every minute of it; wouldn't have missed it for the world."

But when she does leave I know she will take with her the
heartfelt appreciation and respect of thousands of lads of India's
Fourteenth Army.

All best wishes, Vera Lynn, and thanks a million.

* * *

back slightly from a spot very, very close to the action zone — so close, in fact, that Len Edwards, [her] celebrated accompanist, was wishing that he had brought along a good, loud grand piano to drown the bangs, instead of a tiny, gentle, pianissimo job he is carrying around in his waistcoat pocket.

But Vera — bless her golden tonsils — so tired in the midst of so strenuous a tour, had to be awakened so that she could listen.

She is going forward again in a couple of days but, of course, her exact destinations must be confidential, if not a military secret; from a morale standpoint she is the best little thing that ever happened out here. If you doubt it listen to the applause.

Vera still has a lot of performances before she considers her tour complete, and she will have to crowd them into a very short space of time for she is returning to England in a few weeks to keep a date with a picture at Columbia Studios.

'And thanks a lot for everything,' she says, 'I've enjoyed every minute of it; wouldn't have missed it for the world.'

But when she does leave I know she will take with her the heartfelt appreciation and respect of thousands of lads of India's Fourteenth Army.

All best wishes, Vera Lynn, and thanks a million.

Interestingly, although Ma noted in her diary that she had gone as far south as Elephant Point at the mouth of the Rangoon River, a claim repeated in various places over the years, I cannot see how this could have been the case, as Elephant Point and Rangoon were held by the Japanese almost up until the end of the war in 1945. I realised that Ma instead must have gone to the mouth of the Naf River, where there is a settlement called Teknaf, not far from where she had sung at Bawli Bazar the previous day. There are some wonderful photographs of her at the seaside there, wearing a bikini and looking happy and carefree far away from the fighting. More importantly, the men who are with her also look like they are having a wonderful time and have forgotten their troubles.

There is one rather amusing story that was sent to Ma in 2012 that relates to a performance she gave at Bawli Bazar. Sergeant Arthur Webberley of the 1st Somerset Company Regimental Police told the story of how his friend managed to get my mother's autograph.

Whilst based at Bawli Bazar we were entertained by a touring concert party that had as its star — the forces' sweetheart — the one and only Dame Vera Lynn. Ern — known as the smart crafty lad from Somerset — has recorded how using his initiative against all the odds managed to secure Dame Vera's autograph.

I would like to read you a shortened version of how his ruse paid off.

After sitting with approximately 1,000 troops and thoroughly enjoyed the show the sergeant in charge of the concert party announced that anyone with a decent piece of paper or suitable item was welcome to stand in an orderly queue to receive an autograph.

Due to where we were sited Ern quickly

145

ascertained that there was no way he would be receiving an autograph on the 10 rupee note he had in his pocket. Quick as a flash Ern removed his jacket, vest and one shoe. He fashioned a bandage, made from his vest, put it around his foot, put his jacket back on, stuffed his shoe in the pocket of his jacket and then using myself and Bill as supports Ern directed us to the head of the queue. The sergeant in charge was just about to blow his top when he spotted Ern's bandaged foot . . . the sgt thrust out his regimental cane to the next lad in the queue shouting hang on, hang on, hang on, and beckoned us forward for Ern to receive his autograph which Dame Vera kindly did. Ern thanked the sergeant profusely and with the help of his supports trundled back up the incline laughing our heads off.

While not condoning queue jumping moments like these with men like Ern helped maintain morale and spirits during what was a very difficult time.

Soon after he took over as the commander of the Fourteenth Army, Slim had moved the army headquarters from Barrackpore, on the outskirts of Calcutta, much closer to the Burmese border. He hated Barrackpore, its 'sordid slums' and the 'faded splendour of the pre-mutiny buildings in which we worked and lived'. He also felt that the distractions of Calcutta, which may have been positive for the fighting troops back from the front line, were a positive hindrance to his administrative staff. Worst of all, Barrackpore was simply too far away from the front line — Imphal was around 400 miles away, for

Outside the ENSA office in my rather stiff ENSA uniform with a pleated skirt.

Me with Lieutenant General Walter Lentaigne.

There were all sorts of unfamiliar sights, smells and sounds on my travels – from Indian markets (like this one) to the Egyptian pyramids.

As anyone knows who has done much travelling, you generally spend as much time waiting to leave as you do on the road.

My khaki shorts were a constant companion – they were perfect during the day in the hot weather, but I had to cover up in the evenings because of the mosquitoes.

With the convalescing troops of the 81st West African Division on 26 April, on my way south down the Arakan Road.

Some members of the government thought it was inappropriate for me to perform for the troops without a chaperone, but I had grown up singing in working men's clubs and was used to it.

This was actually one of the more formal theatres – I more often sang out in the open on the back of trucks and on aeroplane engine boxes, and inside tents and bamboo huts.

Below: Here I am bowing to applauding, wounded men – note the bandage around the man's head in the foreground.

Above: A rare outing for the dress that I brought with me from England and, I think, a shawl that I picked up in India.

My performances were not amongst the most glamorous of my career – long trousers and buttoned-down shirt sleeves against a backdrop of bedsheets made sure of that.

The men were always so welcoming when I came to perform, often giving me presents such as these beautiful jungle flowers – wrapped in surgical gauze!

It is hard to appreciate just how remote some of the camps I visited were – the men sometimes felt that they really were in the middle of nowhere.

I may have been sitting on this motorbike, but I can assure you that I wasn't riding it! The boys in the jeep next to me look amused.

Neville Hogan stealing a kiss and putting a smile on everybody's faces!

The Fourteenth Army really was a melting pot of different nationalities – Gurkhas, Indians, Africans and others all played their parts, as well as the Brits.

Signing autographs seemed as popular amongst the men as singing and my arm was almost as tired as my voice by the end of the tour.

TONIGHT @ 20-30 HRS
11-4-44

Someone designed this lovely poster for my performance at an anti-aircraft guns site near Calcutta on 11 April 1944.

Palms, banana trees and grass-roofed huts were common sights in the army camps and airfields where I performed all the way along the Indo-Burmese border.

I didn't see many other women from home but there were
a handful of nurses in a few of the casualty clearing stations
on the outskirts of the jungle doing amazing work.

Near the mouth of the Naf River, after a swim in the gorgeous
Andaman Sea.

I have the feeling that this ride in a pulled rickshaw in Calcutta was a photo opportunity rather than part of a real journey through the city.

The distinctive bush – or slouch – hats were worn by Chindits in the Fourteenth Army.

Facing page: Back in England, it was as if nothing had changed and yet everything was different for me.

Sergeant Horace Powell (*left*) and his brother Ronald (*centre*), both of the Royal Welsh Fusiliers, came to see me sing near Chittagong.

Although I had my cryptic notes in my Collins diary, the photographs from my time in Burma are real treasures to me.

When our London home was damaged in a landmine, Harry and I decided to move out of London.

Without making any formal announcement, I devoted the next couple of years of my life to having a family. Virginia was born in 1946.

After the war, life didn't really slow down. Here I have been awarded a doctorate of laws by Memorial University of Newfoundland.

Ginny: Squadron Leader Tom Jones, we married happily in 1986.

Whilst out in Burma, being away from loved ones was one of the hardest things to deal with. It really taught me to appreciate time together as a family: Virginia, myself and my son-in-law Tom at home.

Virginia, Tom and I at home, after I was awarded the Order of the Companions of Honour in the Queen's Birthday Honours list in 2016.

instance. So he chose Comilla, which had relatively good road and rail links, the capability to be turned into an air centre, and a reasonable number of administrative buildings. The move began in October 1943, and so when my mother arrived there, it was still a relatively new base.

On 5 May, just a few days after swimming in the warm waters of the Bay of Bengal, Ma was singing for the junior ranks mess in Comilla, a fact that a letter written to her the following day was keen to remind her of.

Dear Vera and Len,

We are wondering if you can remember just where you were at approximately 1300 hrs, better known to you perhaps as 1 o'clock, on the 5th May 1944?

It was at this time and on the day mentioned that we had the pleasure of your company in our mess, and though this was only for a few short minutes it was greatly welcomed. How really grand it was to see a 'Real Bit' of England once again. Actually we all owe you sincere apologies for not showing any outward signs of pleasure in seeing you, but you can rest assured this was due to 'shyness' and for this we can but ask forgiveness. Whatever else though in our hearts we more than welcomed you and greatly appreciate your kindness in favouring us with a visit. Seeing that most of us here have been in this country for well over two years now, we can appreciate the great discomfort you have undergone during your tour and we trust that this will have no after effects.

Yours is a great and arduous task and you have come through with flying colours.

We can say no more than THANKS and thanks again, but we really do mean it.

So, cheerio for now, here's to the time when we shall all meet again, may it be very soon and of course in England.

With one accord we wish you the best of good luck and every success in the future.

Very sincerely yours,

Members of junior ranks mess

On 10 May, she sang at the RAF base at Agartala. One of the men who watched her perform was Thomas Nutt, of 31 Squadron. He remembered that:

It was probably about April or May 1944 that we had a visit from the forces' sweetheart, Vera Lynn. We were then stationed at Agartala, not far from the Burma border. This visit was very important. She spent the whole day in the camp, having a midday meal with us in the dining room. We had photographs taken with her afterwards and in the evening she sang the old songs we loved. The two favourites were 'We'll Meet Again' and 'The White Cliffs of Dover'. It was a great morale boost and as well as that many of us hadn't seen a white woman in months.

Clifford Woodcock, a member of the aircrew at Agartala, remembered that the airfield was built on the only truly flat ground in the area and was surrounded by scrub and small patches of jungle. Most of the rest of the jungle had been cleared to make way for rice paddy, and the surrounding hillsides had also been terraced for growing rice. There was a football pitch at one end of the airstrip, which the men used a lot in the evenings before the weather got too hot. He wrote:

On the entertainment front we were reasonably well served with a visit from a section of the Devonshire Regiment's Band. The highlight for me, though, was a visit from Vera Lynn. We were given half a day off in order to attend this concert and were entertained to many of the 'old favourites' as well as newer material. The atmosphere was highly charged, even if we were sitting outside for an open-air concert. At the end of the show, I — along with a few others — managed to get her autograph. This was written on a 1 rupee note and is reproduced below from the original that I still have in my album and I want to record thanks here to a great lady who helped boost our morale during a very depressed period in our fortunes.

Bert Thomas was also there, and he wrote a lovely letter to Ma in 2012, in which he remembered the occasion very clearly.

Dear Vera,
Please excuse me for being personal (using your Christian name) but being an old 'Burma Boy' I look upon you as one of the family.
We have met and it's a day I and my pals will never forget. It was 10 May 1944, the day you visited my squadron (31 Sqdn) at RAF Station

149

Agartala on the Burma front.

You flew in to our camp in one of our Dakota planes and was accompanied by one of our officers. I and one of my RAF police colleagues were on duty at the entrance to the domestic camp and you kindly agreed to have some photos taken.

Although a special lunch had been arranged for you in the officers' mess, you insisted on having lunch with the boys in an old 'bashar' which we called your cookhouse.

It was a particularly hot day and because of your presence the cookhouse was a bit crowded. Some of us hadn't seen a white girl (let alone the famous Vera Lynn) for several years but you took time to sign autographs for all of us.

After lunch, with my old 'box' camera I took some more photos including some groups, one of which has been used in several books.

One of the interesting things about this story is that it records how Ma passed on the opportunity to have lunch in the officers' mess, preferring instead to eat with the ranks, in much more humble conditions. I think that says a lot. She was loved by the men and was not foisted upon them by the top brass in an attempt to improve their morale. She mentions elsewhere that at some of her shows, seats were reserved for officers at the front, and if they were late in turning up, she would tell the rank-and-file men to move forward and fill the seats.

I think Ma got on well with all kinds of people — and she counted General Slim as a friend — but in the same way that the BBC for a time railed against her music as 'slush', I think there were elements in the senior ranks of the army and air force who didn't like the emotional content of her songs, and who thought it was effeminate for fighting men to listen to lyrics about love and being away from home. My mother wrote about it in her autobiography:

> *Certain belligerent MPs and high-ranking retired military officers — none of whom was actually doing any of the fighting — jumped to the conclusion that a sentimental song produced sentimental soldiers, who would become home-sick and desert at the first catch in a crooner's voice. What the boys were presumed to need was more martial stuff — a view that completely overlooked the experience of a previous world war, which, as it got grimmer, produced steadily more wistful songs. As I saw it, I was reminding the boys of what they were really fighting for, the precious personal connections rather than the ideologies and theories.*

Also there at the RAF base on 10 May was Leading Aircraftman Bartledge. His wife at home in England sent a note of appreciation when she heard from her husband that he had watched Ma sing to him and the rest of the RAF boys.

> *I was pleased to know that you had arrived safely back in the old country. My husband wrote to say that he heard you sing when you visited their RAF station the first week in May, and that he admired you for going out there in the deadly heat to sing to the lads. I would like to ask a favour of you, if*

you should be broadcasting to the forces in India would you please sing 'Journey's End in Lovers' Meeting' for our 6th wedding anniversary on September 24. The best of luck in the great work you are doing.

Remarkably enough, almost seventy years after her father saw my mother singing at the cinema in Agartala, and wrote to thank her, Harry Procter's daughter Avril wrote to Ma to tell her that she had discovered a photo while going through his papers.

I came across a photograph of you that you had signed for him on 10th May 1944.

On the back of the photograph (which I am keeping) he had written a rather touching record of what happened. I have photocopied the photograph and also what he had written on the back of the photo.

He was serving in the RAF.

I think it is wonderful to know how much you were appreciated all those years ago.

The inscription on the back of the photograph reads:

Given to me on May 10 by Vera Lynn in the forward area at a camp called Agartala. She was exceptionally good and the poor kid was simply ringing [sic] wet through with perspiration. She went straight outside the cinema and signed autographs (mostly on one rupee notes), hundreds of them. God bless her always, and protect her safely back to England.

H. Procter

The day before Harry Procter heard Ma sing in Agartala, Private A. E. Dyson of the 14th Infantry Brigade was among the audience at one of the two shows that she did for the army in Comilla. He wrote:

I appreciated very much of your singing to the troops this evening, I certainly did like to hear your voice and for your giving this entertainment, for the first time for many years and I certainly hope it will not be the last; for the first time I heard you sing was in the pictures and especially you sang one of my favourites which were 'Yours' which I were very pleased to hear for I sent this tune 'Yours' to my wife many months ago and now I send you my heartiest congratulations throughout your tour of India and wish you more successes and a speedy return back to your and our home country merry England. CHEERIO AND THE BEST OF LUCK. Hope to hear you again in England when hostilities are over on the films.

While Ma was heading northwards up the Indo-Burmese border, the fighting at Kohima and Imphal continued. At Kohima, the Japanese attacks on the Allied positions had stopped, but the entrenched Japanese forces were proving difficult to budge. Further south, on the Imphal plain, heavy attacks on 26 April were repelled but the fighting continued. After the failure of direct attacks, the Japanese tried instead to infiltrate British defensive lines. This was something that Slim had prepared the troops for, though. One of his key tactical lessons learned from previous campaigns was that 'All units must get used to having Japanese parties in their rear, and, when this happens, regard not themselves, but the Japanese, as 'surrounded'.'

In those first two weeks of May at Imphal, the Japanese air force attempted to regain the initiative in the skies by bombing and strafing British airfields. Japanese aircraft also attacked the strategically important town of Bishenpur on 6 and 10 May. But the RAF's overall superiority as well as the anti-aircraft defences meant that there were no further aerial attacks, and the ground troops held firm, despite losing a dozen tanks around the village of Potsangbam. Slim noted that at this time, and for the first time, Japanese soldiers had started deserting — 'The fact that even two or three deserters had appeared was a new and encouraging sign,' he later wrote.

What is not clear is how closely my mother was kept updated on the military situation while she was touring around visiting various camps. Of course she did not record any details in her diary, but I feel that she must have had a good idea of what was going on and how tense the entire front was. The most important thing for her was the welfare of the boys, though, and I honestly think that she was too busy entertaining and talking to them to spend much time thinking about the bigger picture.

As the rains swept in and the dirt tracks turned to mud, Ma headed further north still, towards the Himalayan mountains and the Chinese border, but also towards near total exhaustion.

Beetles, Mosquitoes, Leopard Skins and Elephants

Vera

On 12 May, I climbed into a Douglas DC-3 aircraft and headed north to Sylhet, which these days is in Bangladesh but which was then in Assam in India. We arrived just before 2 p.m. and went straight to a hospital there, passing well-tended tea plantations, rice paddies and lush jungle vegetation along the way. I remember that the cases in that hospital were particularly bad; even though I had by then been to many different hospitals, I was still shocked by the severity of them. On a couple of occasions in hospitals the boys would ask me to sing for them right by their bedsides as they were unable to make it to one of my performances — at least twice I sang for my smallest audience of just two; and on both occasions I believe that one of the two men did not make it. One of these times — and it may have been in one of those hospitals near Sylhet — I met a man called Stanley McDermott of the King's Own Scottish Borderers, who was very ill with malaria, and sang to him and another man in a neighbouring bed. Many years later his daughter sent me a letter to tell me that this was 'his proudest memory' from the war.

Perhaps the thing I remember most about my visit to Sylhet, though, was being pestered by insects in the jungle when I was trying to sing to the boys. The most memorable type of insect there was definitely the beetles — they had the misfortune to be both gigantic and clumsy, and ended up getting into all types of places, including my hair and the piano keys! Their favourite trick was to fly straight into a light and then fall on the floor — or the piano. They then made an alarming scratchy sound as they righted themselves and tried to scramble to safety. A number of times a beetle would fly into my hair or land on my shoulder just as I started a song, and it would disturb me so much that I would stop singing, turn to Len, apologise to the audience and have to start again.

In general, though, beetles were not the worst insect problem — that dubious honour definitely belonged to mosquitoes. The main problem with mosquitoes was not the bites themselves, but the danger of malaria, which meant that I could hardly ever wear the sleeveless pink dress that I had brought with me from London. I mainly had to wear khaki trousers and shirts with long sleeves so that I wouldn't get bitten on the arms or legs. On the odd occasion that I was seen in the evenings with my sleeves still rolled up, the boys would yell at me: 'Roll down your sleeves, Vera!' That's why in all the pictures from that time I am always dressed in army fatigues. This, I know, was a big part of General Slim's drive to eliminate malaria as much as possible from the army, and I was happy to follow orders as much for my own benefit as anything else.

It was in Sylhet that I really was singing in the

rain — the monsoon was finally upon us. This meant plenty of squelchy, muddy tracks, in which our truck with the piano on the back occasionally got stuck. There was also mud at the various camps, and occasionally one or more of the most gallant boys would offer to carry me over it to the stage or the canteen. A lady called Rachel Holloway from Ealing in west London wrote to me in 2012 to let me know that her grandfather was one of those men who had helped to pull our vehicle out of the mud.

You were out in Burma cheering up the troops whilst my grandad was serving out there. He told me once about a concert you gave whilst out there. My grandad, Harry, served in the Royal Electrical and Mechanical Engineers. He used to tell a story about when a jeep got stuck in mud and you needed assistance getting out.

In all other respects my grandfather was an immensely private man but he spoke warmly of his comrades in Burma and your efforts with the troops.

I wish you well and wanted to express my thanks for the happiness that you so obviously gave to people, soldiers, in particular, who were so in need of comfort and a connection with home.

On 13 May, after having photographs taken with the boys and being shown a gun display, we did the first of two concerts in Sylhet in the open air. I was told that we were not far away from

Cherrapunjee — known to be the wettest place in the world — and I could well believe it when it started to absolutely hammer it down. I got drenched. We performed the second concert under cover at the football ground, and it was here that I met Brigadier Lentaigne for the first time. He had taken over from General Wingate as the leader of the Chindit forces that went behind the enemy lines.

That night Len and I were put in a concrete outhouse to sleep, with a sheet hung between us for propriety. We were both tired, but we didn't get much sleep. All the time we had been having dinner with the brigadier, there had been torrential rain, which now poured in under the door of our outhouse and soaked us. There was nowhere else to sleep, though, so we just had to get wet and put up with it. You have to remember that when a war is taking place, discomforts like this really seem of so little importance.

We travelled from Sylhet to Shillong on 14 May on a very dangerous and difficult road, which twisted and turned through jungle-covered mountains, sometimes as high as 6,000 feet. It was an extraordinary and exhausting journey and so I was relieved that we did not have to do any entertaining that evening when we arrived. Instead we had a very welcome cup of tea before going to bed early.

Over the next few days we made up for this day of travel and no performances or visits with a number of engagements — at a Toc H convalescent home (run by a Christian organisation founded in Belgium during the First World

162

War), a garrison theatre, an RAF camp and several hospitals. One of the best things about Shillong was the climate — because it was that much higher, it was much cooler than anywhere else we had been, and the evenings were actually a little chilly. For this reason, it was also a popular place for convalescent troops, particularly as wounds tend to heal more quickly in cooler conditions. I was really rather exhausted by this time, and I remember on 16 May General Slim's wife Aileen taking me under her wing and saying to me something along the lines of 'You poor thing, you look exhausted, you must come up to the house and have a cup of tea.' Also taking tea with Mrs Slim that afternoon in her bungalow, Stoneylands, was Major General Ranking, the commander of the base and rear areas of Assam, known as 202 Line of Communication Area. At this time he was under a great deal of strain, as he had been moved from being responsible for mainly administrative duties into an active frontline role, trying to repel the Japanese attack from breaking through into Assam.

Although I generally enjoyed meeting people, from the regular men to the top brass in the army and the RAF, I clearly did not always find every occasion to be entertaining. I recorded in my diary after one evening — most definitely not after spending time with either General Slim or his wife — that I had 'Dinner at club. Bored to tears. Home to bed at 12.00.' You see, I may have been doing my bit, but I wasn't a saint!

On 18 May, I was pleased to see some familiar faces once more: Elsie and Doris Waters, whom I had encountered back in Bombay, were also in Shillong. They were always such fun — in real life as well as on the stage — and it was fantastic to spend even just a little time with them. I did another hospital visit after that and had tea once again with General and Mrs Slim later in the afternoon. After dinner at the mess we met up with Elsie and Doris again back at our bungalow and went to bed at 10.30.

It felt like we had only just arrived in Shillong, but unfortunately by 19 May it was time to move on yet again. I had been enjoying the cool mountain air, and the caring company of Mrs Slim, but now we had to journey another 250 miles north to Jorhat. Up in the north, the American General Joe Stilwell was in charge of Allied soldiers comprising American, Chinese and other troops, though still under the control of General Slim. Jorhat was at the edge of this northern zone. It was an eventful journey — first of all we saw a pair of wild elephants by the roadside, and then, when we stopped at an engineer's mess along the way for lunch, a man called Lieutenant Stockton presented me with a leopard skin. This is now sadly lost, though it remained in my possession for many years, and although I am an animal lover who disapproves of taking skins and furs from animals, it was a poignant reminder of the harshness and beauty of the jungle.

The story of the leopard skin reminds me of another strange story that I heard recently, from Peter Scrivener, whose father George served in Burma with the Royal Artillery.

Like a lot of soldiers who served over there he didn't talk much about it. He did however tell me that he had met you on one of your visits to entertain the troops and you gave him an autograph on a one rupee note.

I still have that one rupee note and it's in very good condition for its age.

Although he didn't say much about the bad things that went on, he did tell an account of snakes that joined the soldiers at night in their foxholes as the men tried to sleep. To the men it was a case of let me get out of here as I don't know what type of snake it is.

Apparently they used to snuggle up to the soldiers for warmth during the cold nights. On one particular occasion a very large python decided to keep my dad company in his foxhole. This was an incentive for a bit of running practice and Dad legged it. As he started to run, Dad drew his kukri and threw it in the general direction of the snake, killing it. He always claimed that the snake must have struck at the kukri as the moon glinted off it. He always denied being good at throwing the weapon.

One of the dhobi boys took the dead snake away and as far as Dad was concerned, that was the end of the matter.

A few days later the troops moved on to a different part of Burma.

Some weeks after that the same dhobi boy found out where the troops had gone and caught up with Dad. The dhobi boy *presented him with the skin of the snake which had been tanned. The measurements of the skin are 85 inches long by 9 inches at the widest part.*

The skin along with the one rupee note were brought home after the war and have been looked after ever since. I still have them. I have been told that a similar skin is in a Sheffield museum but not in as good condition. That is testament to the skills of the dhobi boy in doing such a good job preparing it.

I gathered later from General Slim's son John that elephants were employed by the army during the Burma campaign — he told me that over a thousand were used to help build bridges as the troops made their way deeper and deeper into Burma. Probably the animal I saw the most though was pack mules, which were used to transport supplies through the jungle. Years later I received an extraordinary letter from someone called Captain Jim Hough, who wrote to tell me that I had single-handedly helped to save 400 mules from being shot! Although there may be a grain of truth in there, I'm not entirely sure that all of this story is accurate. You'll see what I mean. Here is the main gist of what he wrote:

We met in early 1944, not far from Imphal. You had called on a Chindit column of which I was a member and gave us one of your memorable concerts. It was a great occasion and, for you, a personal triumph.

Everybody was in high spirits because the Japs were being soundly trounced for the first time and it seemed that the war on our front might soon be over. After an al fresco dinner the officers were lined up to be introduced to you.

In the course of our quite short conversation you were informed that I was an animal officer, in charge of 400 mules. I might have told you that only the previous day I had been involved in swimming and wading many of them across the River Chindwin. You told me that you had been reading about these remarkable animals and how it would have been impossible to win the war without them. You asked me what would happen when we had no further use for them. I had to tell you that it had already been decided that they would be painlessly put down. We would not give them to the native Burmese as we had all witnessed the disregard and cruelty with which domestic animals were treated in Burma. No way would we allow our mules to suffer their fate.

You said that you were appalled to hear this and what a dreadful way to repay these noble animals after their devoted and invaluable service. You are an animal lover and had a good deal to say on the subject.

[. . .]

Later that morning I was attending a meeting of top SEAC officials in a railway carriage. Bill Slim, the Field Marshal,

167

Commander of the 14th Army, was one of the dignitaries present. There was also Major General Arthur Snelling, Chief of the Indian Army, Commander Michael Snelling of the Royal Navy, his son, and others, including a senior RAF officer. I was taking the minutes. A messenger entered, came right up to me and handed me an army telegram form, written in pencil and addressed [to me]. It was from the Cabinet Office, London SW1. The message was brief and unequivocal. DO NOT SHOOT MULES. CHURCHILL.

The implication is that I used my influence to contact Churchill to tell him to save the mules. It is a wonderful story, and of course if I had had a hotline to Winston Churchill then I might have used it a number of times for various things, but I am fairly certain that even if I could have spoken to him on the telephone, he probably at that point, just a couple of weeks before D-Day, had more important things to worry about than a few hundred mules in Burma! And in any case, if I had had access to a telephone, I have no doubt that the first person I would have called would have been not Churchill but my husband Harry! I can only think that the author of this letter must have been mistaken and that the order to save the mules had come from elsewhere. Regardless, I am pleased that the mules could be saved, and it is always good in wartime to find a happy story rather than a tragic one.

We set off again after lunch and arrived at Jorhat at 8 p.m. I had a bath and dinner, then went to bed. The following morning I enjoyed the relatively rare luxuries of washing my hair (which in the humidity had become permanently curled) and reading a book, before I gave a lunchtime concert to a Plantation Club audience of 2,000 and, later, went to a dinner somewhere where I was the only woman present.

At some point over the next couple of days we headed even further north, closer to Stilwell's northern front, and stopped in at a hospital at Dibrugarh on the wide Brahmaputra River, where a man called Neville Hogan, who was in the Chindits, gave me a rather memorable kiss on the cheek. I say memorable, because some sixty years later it was repeated — a story that I'll return to later on in the book. Neville had just come back from behind enemy lines, where he had contracted typhus from a rat bite in the jungle while he was asleep. At the time, there was no known cure. He was airlifted out and taken straight to the hospital. The man in the bed next to him was Major Archibald Wavell, son of General Wavell; Neville told me that Wavell had been reading *The Hound of the Baskervilles* by Arthur Conan Doyle to him as he tried to recover from the disease. He said that he never wanted to read that book ever again!

After a couple of days in the north, I made my way on to the Manipur Road for the trip to Dimapur — an important supply station just behind the front line, near where the brutal battles of Kohima and Imphal were being fought at that very time. It was the final stop of my tour of Burma, and by the time I arrived there, I felt that I was at the very centre of where the most crucial battle of the entire conflict was reaching its bloody conclusion.

Ginny

Right from the beginning of her trip, my mother appreciated that the hospital visits, the impromptu autograph sessions and the chats with the men in jungle clearings and canteens were just as important as her actual performances on the stage. After the intense fighting in April and the beginning of May, the hospitals behind the front line were full of casualties being taken out of Kohima and Imphal. Her presence was important not only for the wounded men, but also for those men who were still fighting, who heard of her hospital visits and felt glad that their fallen comrades had not been forgotten. Private Jack Pottrell wrote: 'On behalf of all my comrades, I would like to show how deeply grateful we all are for the lovely soothing, healing quality of your voice.' Taking care of the men properly was a key part of Slim's strategy, and the men in the Fourteenth respected that. They thought of Slim, who came from a relatively humble background, as one of their own, a soldier's general, in the same way that they thought of my mother as one of their own.

One of the people Ma met while visiting the many hospitals on this trip was Ken Dix, who in 1944 was an armourer in the RAF. His son Barry wrote to my mother in 2012 describing how his dad had suffered from an eye infection similar to impetigo and was hospitalised. The treatment meant that he had both of his eyes covered by bandages and was unable to see for some time.

On one of the mornings he became aware of a lot of excitement going on and suddenly heard a female voice asking what the problem was and how long he would have the bandages over his eyes. She said she hoped he would soon be all right again and said goodbye. Unaware of who it was, he asked the chap in the next bed, to be told: 'That was Vera Lynn!' So dad met you but never saw you!

He did eventually manage to see Ma properly, quite a few years later, but that's a story for the final chapter of this book.

A similar reunion also took place between Ma and Major Neville Hogan, the Chindit who kissed her on the cheek at Dibrugarh. Hogan was born in what was then Rangoon (now Yangon) in 1923. His father was an Irishman working for the Irrawaddy Shipping Company and his mother was a schoolteacher from one of the Karen hill tribes. Karen villages often suffered when the Burma Independence Army collaborated with the Japanese during the Japanese invasion of the country. This was one of the reasons why the Karen people largely sided with the British. Hogan enlisted into the local Rangoon-Burma Auxiliary Force at the age of sixteen and saw action on the long retreat out of Burma into India. After the retreat, he received his officer training in Dehra Dun in northern India and fought with the King's Own Rifles, 111th Brigade — one of the brigades that made up the Chindit forces, first under General Wingate and then under General Lentaigne. In 1946, at the age of twenty-three, he would become the army's youngest major, serving in the 2nd Battalion Burmese Rifles.

In 1943, Hogan was sent down the Chindwin River to try to help survivors from the first Chindit expedition behind enemy lines. However, they had all either been killed or captured. He was then part of the second Chindit expedition, which flew behind enemy lines by glider on the night of 5 March 1944. There were four landing areas that had been identified in clearings in the jungle and given the codenames Aberdeen, Piccadilly, Broadway and Chowringhee. They were all away from roads and inhabited areas; there was enough flat ground to land on and water nearby for the troops to fill up their canteens. The 111th Brigade, with Hogan amongst them, was sent in to Broadway. But disaster struck immediately when some of the gliders crash-landed, killing many men. One or two of the leading gliders, descending in the darkness and circling down to the clearing, crashed on landing. Some of the following gliders slammed into the wreckage, while others smashed into the trees or were flipped over by concealed bumps in the ground and destroyed. Twenty-three men were killed and many injured, but over 400 survived and continued with the operation.

Surviving the landing was just the first of a whole series of incredible challenges for the Chindits as they tried to disrupt the Japanese offensive at Imphal. They had to carry large packs, the humidity was crushing and some men even broke their ankles in knee-deep elephant tracks in swampy ground. When they engaged with the enemy, the fighting was fierce. There was relatively little food and an abundance of malarial

173

mosquitoes. After contracting typhus from rat bites, Hogan was evacuated to safety and woke up seriously ill in hospital at Dibrugarh.

When Ma stopped at his bedside during a tour of the hospital, she asked if there was anything she could do for him. 'I asked for a kiss,' said Hogan, 'and she kindly obliged.'

Other ex-Chindits got in touch with Ma to tell her that they had seen her perform in Burma too. They included Private C. Stephens from Birmingham, who wrote to her in October 1944.

Whilst serving in Burma with the 'Chindits' I was unfortunately evacuated out of the field with BT malaria and sent to the BMH Shillong (Assam) after being sent to a convalescence camp. Miss Vera Lynn gave us a concert which was most delightful. After the show I happened to strike lucky enough to be in the front row when we were snapped. Now I was wondering if I enclose a photograph of myself to enable Miss Lynn to send me a copy of one of those photographs, I would be very happy. So would you convey my thanks on behalf of my comrades who are left back, how much we like her, and feel quite grateful that Miss Lynn should go through discomforts to cheer us all.

There were other men who may not have been in the Chindits but whose job it was to help support them. Trevor Cowls was in the RAF; he wrote to Ma in 2010.

Whilst going through some old papers I came across a photo of the open-air cinema, located on the USA-operated airfield near Sylhet, in Assam, from which 117 Transport Squadron RAF was operating whilst supporting the Wingate columns behind the Jap lines and our own forces defending Imphal against the Jap attack.

I remember that you came to the cinema one hot humid evening and sang to us and that before the end of your concert your clothes were wet with perspiration and you still sang on! How we enjoyed your concert. Very few artistes followed in your footsteps.

I thought that you might like to have a copy of the photo of the cinema and so have included two copies and would be much obliged if you would be kind enough to sign one copy and return it to me.

With every best wish and happy memories of that night.

In another recent letter, A. B. Evans remembered the insects flying into Ma in Sylhet.

I am 93 years old and suffer the odd senior moment, but each time I listen to one of my Vera Lynn CDs, I am reminded of the evening when she sang to our group during her Burma tour in 1944. It was soon after Gen. Wingate had been killed in an air crash. His successor Gen. Lentaigne introduced both Vera and himself to us. For a long time afterwards her visit was the subject of many conversations.

I was one of a small REME unit living and working in some former paddy fields, nearby we had the signal corps keeping in touch with the

Chindit columns operating behind Japanese lines. Any request for food or equipment was passed on to the RASC who had stocks of just about everything needed. They were helped by a team fitting items into parachutes ready for a 'drop'. The US air force nearby were responsible for that part of the operation.

One incident during our evening occurred as Vera was about to hit a high note — one of our many flying insects hit her on the cheek. She gave a shriek and said — 'I think I should start again.' In her autobiography she said that the hut she was given at Sylhet became flooded during a thunderstorm. I have often thought that maybe that same storm flooded our hut.

Eric Deacon had some similar memories:

I was stationed at Sylhet in Assam near the Burma border, serving in the Signal Section of III India Infantry Brigade, part of General Wingate's LRP Group (Chindits). When you gave a concert on an American stage nearby on May 24th 1944 we were thrilled to be in a position [to see it]. It was in the bush and all sorts of weird insects were flying about and you had to keep knocking them away from your mouth so you could sing. You very kindly gave me your autograph which I still have as a memento to remind me how lucky I am to be alive as a lot of my group did go in as reinforcements and never came back, the tide had just turned by then and the Japanese were retreating from northern Burma.

Now travelling further forward in time I was

introduced to you at a concert given by Ron Goodwin at Enfield, London, on July 1st 2000 commemorating the 60th anniversary of the Battle of Britain. The music of those dance band days is still with me which I avidly listened to as a teenager, it certainly kept us going in the forces.

I am now an 89-year-old widower living on my own with memories of years gone by.

My mother reached the most northerly part of her journey along the front when she got to Jorhat. Slim wrote that:

The northern was the most isolated of the Burma fronts. To reach it by rail — there was no road — you left Dimapur and continued your seemingly interminable journey through the tea-garden area of Assam. As you crept northward, it was impossible to avoid a growing feeling of loneliness, which even the sight of the increasingly busy airfields of the Hump route, strung along the line, failed to dissipate.

One of Slim's great challenges was to be a diplomat as well as a soldier. He had to hold together a broad coalition made out of Chinese and Americans in the north, and further south, British, Indian, Burmese, Nepalese and African troops. What made it particularly difficult was the fact that the different nationalities were fighting in different parts of the front — they were segregated from one another and this meant that they did not necessarily always appreciate each other's efforts. As Slim put it: 'The British could not see the Americans and Chinese

177

fighting and enduring in the Hukawng Valley, any more than the Americans could see us waging desperate battles in Imphal and Arakan.'

There were certainly tensions between the Chindits and the American and Chinese coalition on the northern front. On one occasion, the Chindits were being supported by bombing raids delivered by the Chinese, but instead of flying in across the front of the Chindit position, the aircraft came from behind and the bombs narrowly missed the troops on the ground. In general, though, the air support was well coordinated and the US Air Force and the RAF worked closely together to drop provisions at Kohima, Imphal and behind enemy lines to Chindit expeditions. These were absolutely essential to the success of the Allies, especially in remote, inaccessible locations such as Kohima. The drops at Kohima were especially difficult because of the steep hillsides and ridges, and the proximity of the troops to one another. It meant that the pilots had to be highly accurate, while facing enemy small-arms fire. Warrant Officer Colin Lynch of 31 Squadron would fly up in his Dakota from Agartala sometimes twice a day to do these drops.

You could see the road from Dimapur snaking up the valley to the mountains and at the top, at 5,000 feet, there's the Kohima Ridge, not quite a mile long. Where the road turns right and runs along the ridge and off down to Imphal, there's a whole lot of hillocks, and in the middle of those you could see Kojima hill station — or what was left of it.

On both sides of the ridge, the mountains rise up another thousand feet or so and that's where

178

the Japs were, lobbing their shells and mortar bombs into our troops. We had to run the gauntlet to make a drop. There'd usually be a line of Daks going in, one after the other. We dropped them everything you could think of — but mostly ammo, rations and medical supplies.

The American general Joe Stilwell, in command of the northern troops, was a notoriously abrasive character, who was nicknamed 'Vinegar Joe' because of his rather acidic disposition. The Americans in general were suspicious of the British motives in Asia and it was a standing joke amongst them that SEAC — the South East Asian Command — actually stood for 'Saving England's Asian Colonies'. The Americans by contrast were prioritising relations with the Chinese and saw strategic importance in making sure northern Burma was opened up to create a highway through to China. At that point, remember, before the victory of Chairman Mao in 1949, America was actively encouraging China to take a bigger role on the world stage and act as a counter to the old colonial powers. Fortunately, Stilwell had a good relationship with Slim, but his relations with other senior commanders were not always so harmonious.

The eccentric and idiosyncratic Chindit commander General Wingate was also a divisive figure — 'Very few could regard him dispassionately,' wrote Slim — and he accordingly had detractors as well as admirers. One tribute in the *Manchester Guardian* after his death on 24 March stated that 'the country has lost a soldier of genius', and Churchill himself regarded him as a heroic soldier. The tribute continued:

179

He did not coddle anyone: intense, passionate, efficient, and wholly absorbed in his work, he made the highest demands on himself and on others. He had remarkable powers of physical endurance (a brilliant horseman, he had a collection of cups won in point-to-point races). Service under him was not easy, but it was an honour. The men themselves realised what he was making of them; he raised them to levels they could otherwise not attain.

It was Slim's job to choose Wingate's successor. He later reflected on Wingate's legacy and some of the things he had to consider as he decided on who would take over the leadership of the Chindit forces.

There could be no question of the seriousness of our loss. Without [Wingate's] presence to animate it, Special Force [the Chindits] would no longer be the same to others or to itself. He had created, inspired, defended it, and given it confidence; it was the offspring of his vivid imagination and his ruthless energy. It had no other parent. Now it was orphaned, and I was faced with the immediate problem of appointing a successor.

Slim chose Brigadier Walter Lentaigne, who Ma met in Sylhet on 13 May, and who Slim called 'the most balanced and experienced of Wingate's commanders'. A number of other men came forward from the Chindits to say that Wingate had told each one of them that he should be his successor should one be required. For Slim, this was 'an interesting sidelight on the strange personality' of Wingate, as he had no

180

doubt that all of these men who claimed to have been identified as Wingate's heir were telling the truth.

Walter Lentaigne, often known simply as 'Joe', was born in 1899 and joined the British Indian Army as a second lieutenant in 1918, serving in the 4th Gurkha Rifles. He first saw action in the Third Anglo-Afghan war, in 1919. In the Second World War he operated in relatively obscure roles — first as a quartermaster and then as an instructor — before taking command in 1942 of the 1st Battalion, 4th Gurkha Rifles as they fought the Japanese on the retreat out of Burma. Here he demonstrated his personal bravery in a number of close-quarter fights, and in 1943 he formed and took command of 111th Indian Infantry Brigade, which became part of the Chindit long-range penetration (LRP) brigades. Neville Hogan, then a lieutenant, was one of his officers as they flew in behind enemy lines onto the Broadway landing strip at the beginning of March 1944.

Only a few weeks after that, following Wingate's death, Lentaigne was appointed by Slim to take charge of all the Chindit brigades. As Ma had dinner with him in the pouring rain in Sylhet, Lentaigne's troops were under heavy attack, desperately holding on to a position behind enemy lines. Just a few days later, on 17 May, responsibility for the Chindit force was passed from Lentaigne to Stilwell, and though they remained in action for a few more months, it effectively signalled the end of the force that Wingate had originally assembled.

It amazes me how many of Slim's responsibilities at this time were administrative and diplomatic — but I suppose this is all part of the bigger project of waging war. As someone who knows relatively little of military history and strategy, it strikes me that one of Slim's great strengths was the fact that he left no stone unturned in trying to make his army a better fighting operation — and plenty of the detail was not actually to do with the fighting but with everything else that needed to fall into place so that the men had the right equipment, the right rations and were led by the right people. I am still astonished that he managed to find time to sit and have a cup of tea with his wife Aileen and Ma at the Slim family bungalow in Shillong as the battles raged at Imphal and Kohima.

Quite recently I had a coffee with Slim's son, Viscount Slim, who is ten years younger than my mother. During the war he was doing officer training in Dehra Dun in northern India, and he would sometimes go to Burma to see his mother and father. He remembers his mother telling him about the time that Ma arrived in Shillong, and saying, 'That girl would have collapsed at the rate she was going.' I know she was thoroughly exhausted by that time and that she appreciated the care and kindness extended by Mrs Slim. And of course, as they were in north-eastern India, they had the best tea in the world. She not only had tea there, but also stayed in the bungalow as well, and I know she was well taken care of.

* * *

As the monsoon rains came sweeping in, the already difficult situation across the front became even harder as mud, mould, damp and rust took a hold on army equipment, making it more difficult to get anywhere or do even the most basic things that an army has to do.

A rhyme that was popular in the army at the time went:

> *Eck dum, eck dum, the monsoon's come*
> *The bashar walls are drawn*
> *When strong men mutter, grim and glum*
> *'We'll all be drowned by dawn.'*
>
> *Eck dum, eck dum, the monsoon's come*
> *No use to sigh and sob!*
> *Just fill the mugs with char, old pal*
> *And talk about demob.*

Especially in these treacherous conditions for motorised vehicles, mules were a vital form of transportation across thickly forested, steep muddy hills. Some of the men knew them as 'the trucks of the jungle'. Reading Ma's account of this time, I am struck in particular by the story of the mules that she is said to have saved. I share her incredulity about the finer details of the story, but I think it is important to recognise how vital the muleteers were across the Burma theatre — they were able to provide the men with water, tins of bully beef and ammunition in the most remote places, where even air drops were difficult.

In Kohima and Imphal at this time, the fighting continued to be fierce, but from 13 May, when Ma was in Sylhet, the Allied forces made a significant breakthrough at Kohima and started to clear the ridge of enemy forces. Japanese soldiers were seen running off the hillside trying to find cover, and their resistance seemed to be crumbling. The British troops were able to eat a proper meal and survey the utter devastation that the battle had inflicted on what had previously been thick jungle. Now there was barely a blade of grass left, let alone any trees. Instead, the hillside was covered with blackened stumps, shell holes, and all kinds of debris, including the horrendous spectacle of hundreds of half-buried putrid bodies. Captain Michael Lowry wrote: 'The desolation was augmented by millions of flies as they tried to do justice to the feast that 'civilised' man had delivered to them, moving from corpses to latrines, then to our food.'

Even though the worst of the battle seemed to be over, there was much more fighting still to be done. On 18 May, Lowry reports that there was 'very heavy firing'. That night there was a large-scale counter-attack; the fighting across the whole front went on until midnight and gradually petered out in the early hours of the 19th.

By 20 May, Lowry reported that 'although the centre of Kohima Ridge had been cleared of the Japanese, they clung determinedly to their positions in apparent strength on the extreme flanks of the ridge, in the Naga village area to the north and to the south on Aradura Spur about three miles away'. Of all the armies in the world, the Japanese were perhaps the best at defending a position, because they were so unwilling to surrender. Lieutenant Trevor Highett, who was at Kohima, wrote:

The Japanese were magnificent in defence. Every army in the world talks about holding positions to the last man. Virtually no other army, including the Germans, ever did, but the Japs did. Their positions were very well sited and they had a good eye for the ground. They relied on rushing and shouting in the attack. We thought they were formidable fighting insects and savages. We took few prisoners, about one or two in the whole war. We wanted prisoners for information, but wounded men would have a primed grenade under them, so stretcher-bearers were very careful.

On 21 May, my mother arrived in nearby Dimapur, the final destination on her journey along the front line, and the place closest to the most intense and most strategically vital battles of the entire Burma campaign.

Mud, Mortars, Malaria . . . and Whiskey by the River

Vera

Looking back on it now, I think perhaps I should have been a little nervous heading down the Manipur Road to Dimapur on the morning of 21 May, but the truth is that I never had anything less than total confidence in the men who were looking after me, regardless of the military situation that might have been going on at the time. Simply put, they would never have let any harm come to me. The drive took around five hours, along a mainly flat road, down a broad valley with green forested mountains rising up to the east, alongside the Dhansiri River, which carried the monsoon rain south. I remember that we arrived at Dimapur at about 3 p.m. for a late lunch. It was a rather drab, featureless place, made even more so by the dampness and mud that by then, after just a few days of torrential outbursts, seemed to be everywhere. Dimapur was absolutely alive with troops, trucks and activity coming and going, and I felt when I arrived that I was at the very centre of the war effort in Burma. That night I did a performance there. It was extremely muddy, and one of the boys was kind enough to carry me over the worst of the mud and up onto the temporary stage that had been set up for me to sing from.

After the performance that night, I met two war correspondents called Richard Sharp and Gerald Hanley — I simply called them Dick and Gerry. Dick was the BBC correspondent in Burma and Gerry was an army captain also working as a journalist. These days we would say that he was 'embedded' with the 11th East African Infantry Division, and he later wrote a fantastic book called *Monsoon Victory*, based on his experiences. Even though I was only there for three or four days in total, Dimapur is probably the place I think about the most when I remember my trip to Burma. I think that is mainly because some particularly striking things happened to me there.

Dimapur was on the Dhansiri River, and we stayed in a *bashar* behind a high wire fence by the water's edge. We ate our meals on the veranda there when it wasn't raining. It sounds like, were it not for the wire fence, it might have been quite idyllic. But there was one major problem that prevented it from being so, and again it was insect-related. The flies by the river were horrendous, and they descended in great clouds when we ate our dinner. Although the people in the services may object to this kind of language, resistance was simply futile — there was absolutely nothing you could do to get rid of them. I remember eating soup out there on the veranda and there was a knack to doing it without getting a mouthful of flies, which involved scooping in a quick sideways movement. It was quite as revolting as it sounds. At night I tucked myself in under the mosquito net and listened as bush rats ran about above me in the roof.

Dick and Gerry, being the worldly journalists they were, made light of all the various discomforts of life in a tropical war zone. But the one thing that did upset them was the lack of alcohol. I realised that first evening that I was in a position to help. Back in Chittagong, an older officer had given me a bottle of Canadian Club whiskey and said: 'Just a chota peg now and again for medicinal purposes, my dear' — a sentence effectively meaning something like 'A small tot after the sun sinks beneath the yardarm will help you to relax at the end of the day.' Well, I'd lugged that bottle of whiskey all over Burma with me without touching it once, but that evening — 21 May — the time for a chota peg or two was upon us.

Dick and Gerry couldn't believe it when I emerged with a full bottle of whiskey in my hand. There was no soda or ginger ale, so we just sat and drank it neat — the whole thing! I have never been much of a drinker, so you can imagine how much it affected me, in a pleasant, soothing kind of way. The river ran past, swollen and muddy, as we sat and drank. It was the first time that I had slowed down and had the opportunity to properly reflect on what had happened over the past few weeks. I thought about the fighting that was still going on up the hill in Kohima. How peaceful it felt in contrast down here by the river. I suddenly felt extremely tired and made my way carefully to bed, feeling through the darkness in front of me and trying to untangle the mosquito net before laying my heavy head on the pillow.

★ ★ ★

Another episode that has stayed with me when I was at Dimapur was seeing Japanese prisoners up close, sitting on the ground, leaning against my *bashar*. They had obviously just been captured and I physically had to step over them as they sat there. Remember, I was dressed in my khaki shorts, and even the Allied men, most of whom had not seen a Western woman for months or even years, looked at me in some astonishment when they first saw me, as if I couldn't possibly be real. So imagine what those Japanese soldiers thought when I stepped over their legs — they'd probably never even seen a white girl before! They gave me some very curious looks, as if to say: 'What is that woman doing here?' I didn't stop to tell them. But it would have been interesting to hear what their comments to one another were when they saw me — and what their thoughts might have been. I know that not many of them were taken alive: it was a great dishonour for a Japanese soldier to be taken prisoner, and almost all would fight until the death. It meant that many of our boys were also curious about the prisoners, and although they did not talk to me directly about it, I imagine that there was some ill feeling towards them, as the Japanese had become renowned for their brutality in combat, especially to wounded soldiers. The men were also aware of what had been happening to Allied prisoners of war.

On 22 May, I visited three hospitals in one morning and followed those visits with an afternoon and an evening show. The next day I went to two more hospitals. In one of them I also met Lady Mountbatten, the wife of Lord Louis Mountbatten, the Supreme Allied Commander for South East Asian Command. This was during some of the worst of the fighting in the Battle of Kohima, and many of the patients had been terribly wounded, with bad shrapnel injuries and infected wounds. There were moans and cries of pain from the hospital beds. Infections, in the form of gangrene, thrived in those hot, humid conditions, and if you have ever smelled it, you will know that infected, rotting flesh is one of the worst of all smells. Added to the mix were the same clouds of flies that swarmed around our soup down by the river. The medics there were working as hard as they possibly could to save men's lives — and their limbs — and they had a new medicine to help them: penicillin, which at that time was being used in powder form and put straight onto the wound. This of course helped, but there was not much joy in that tent, and I felt a rising nausea and a sense that everything suddenly seemed desperate and futile and awful. I sat down and asked for a glass of water. I was offered some lemonade instead, which turned my stomach even more.

As I sat down, I had a sort of vision — like a daydream. I was transported in my mind to the other side of the world: to Weybourne, near

Farnham, on the border of Hampshire and Surrey. This was the place where we used to go on family holidays from London when I was a child — my mother, my brother Roger and I would spend the whole of August there and my father would join us for some of the time when he could get away from work. Back then it was beautiful, quiet countryside, and for me, coming from the city, it represented a kind of blissful rural idyll. Our holidays there were spent on walks and picnics; an evening stroll across a humpback bridge over the railway to where a lovely old couple called Bill and Annie Walker had a cottage with a well in the garden where we'd stop for a drink of their water. At that moment I wanted a glass of water from that well more than anything else in the world. Sitting on that hospital bed in Dimapur, in the heat and humidity and stench of rotting flesh and dried blood, among the flies and the dirt, I imagined myself drinking that water. It was a strange and poignant moment for me, and one that I have never forgotten. And I have never taken a glass of water for granted since that time.

Normally when I performed at a hospital we would try to fit as many men into a ward as possible and do the concert there. Some men could not be moved, though, and often I would go and sing for those men who were too ill to come to the main performance. I don't think it was the only place where this happened, but in Dimapur I sang to an audience of only two men — Gunner Fred Thomas, from Bootle in Merseyside, and Private John Badger, of

194

Sheffield. Both men had been so badly wounded that they were too ill to be evacuated out of Dimapur, so getting out of bed to hear me sing wasn't an option. So I sang just for the two of them. I still have a tiny little newspaper clipping that I expect my mother had cut out while I was away. It says: 'Vera had tea at their bedsides, chatted about their home towns — and answered a whispered appeal for a song.' They asked me to sing 'We'll Meet Again'. I had a lump in my throat as I was singing it, as slowly and tenderly as I could. In the end, only one of these two boys — Fred Thomas — made it home. Years later, in 1957, I was invited to do *This Is Your Life*, and they had managed to find him. I was so surprised and moved; I couldn't believe it.

On one of those days at Dimapur, Dick and Gerry thought it would be a good idea to take me right up to the front line at Kohima. They wanted to record me with the sound of mortar fire and machine guns in the background. The plan was to leave at dawn and head up into the hills above Dimapur until we heard the noise of the battle up ahead. I naively agreed to the plan, but Dick and Gerry hadn't thought to tell anyone in the army about it. As soon as an officer heard what they intended to do, he gave them a good talking-to. We never made it.

After I was overcome at the hospital on the morning of 23 May, I had one more ordeal to face that day — a much lesser one than in the hospital, admittedly, but one that was shared by everyone who did service in Burma. At dinner with one of the signals units, I tasted for the first

195

time the infamous meat-imitation sausages known as soya links. After I had returned home, I would receive letters that mentioned this staple of the Burma serviceman's diet. 'Hope the memories of the famous 'soya links' do not haunt you too much,' wrote one member of the Royal Engineers; another soldier wrote to me, a little sadly, I felt: 'We are still having soya links.' Following the links we had rice pudding — plain boiled rice with red jam on top of it. While I was eating it, I suddenly found that everyone was looking at me to see if I was having the same as them! Of course I was — there was no à la carte menu available! I think it reassured them that at least everyone was getting the same.

There was very little in the way of luxury in Burma, but although I did hear the men grumbling sometimes, it was always done in a humorous way. I think the worst thing must have been the loneliness and sense of isolation. I got just a small taste of what that must have been like. I missed my husband in particular — as well as the rest of my family — but there was never a time when I wanted to turn around and say 'I've had enough.' I was still happy to be there and I would have stayed for as long as I was allowed to. Nonetheless, it seemed that my time in Burma was drawing to a close. On 24 May, after two morning shows in a hospital, we headed back up the road to Jorhat, ready to begin the arduous trip home.

Ginny

My mother always had absolute faith that she would not come to any harm when she was out in Burma, but the situation around Dimapur was especially volatile at this time, and from my understanding, I think it is quite conceivable that a Japanese patrol could have intercepted Ma on her journey down from Jorhat. Major Morton, who was a member of the Women's Auxiliary Service Burma — the Wasbies — made the same journey in both directions within a couple of weeks of Ma. She remembered that her unit was 'at first housed in Dimapur Transit Camp, but very soon we were moved to Jorhat, about 60 miles north east of Dimapur, where reinforcements had arrived in the shape of 33 Corps, commanded by Lt General Monty Stopford and our canteens immediately began working flat out serving hundreds of troops. Very shortly afterwards a crisis arose, as we were nearly out of stores, the road from Jorhat to Dimapur was threatened by the Japs, and non-operational traffic was banned.'

One soldier who was in hospital in Dimapur was quoted in the newspapers at the time as saying about Ma that 'She was very brave because there were pockets of Japanese all around us.' Of course, if I said that to her she would just laugh and wave me away, as though to say 'Don't be so silly, Ginny.' But the truth is that by 21 May, although the ridge at Kohima had largely been cleared, Japanese troops were widely dispersed through the jungle and the hills above Dimapur. Ma tells the story of the two journalists who tried to take her up to the front line before they were stopped by an officer. However, I did come across one memoir in the Imperial War Museum from someone who claimed that Ma did indeed head into the hills to perform up at Kohima, while fighting was still taking place. Stephen Harwood was in the 4th Battalion Royal West Kent Regiment and had been in the siege in April before being withdrawn down to Dimapur.

We were told to withdraw ... We were taken back down past brigade headquarters and stopped — because that had all been cleared then — and we went down to Dimapur. At Dimapur I'm not too certain what happened because I had malaria.

We went back into Dimapur and I went into hospital — along with others as well. I don't really know what happened in Dimapur over the next week or two.

Dame Vera Lynn came and sang in that hospital — in actual fact she went up to brigade HQ where they were cut off and sang there, but I saw her singing in the hospital.

Ma's own memories of that time are not always distinct, but she does not seem to remember doing this, and without any other corroborating stories, it is difficult to be certain that it did actually happen. Nonetheless, Dimapur was not far away from the main action, and with many of the boys pouring down the hill from the terrible fighting, Ma certainly felt that she

198

was right in the middle of the war.

Elaine Cheverton, another of the Wasbies, remembered Dimapur as 'terrible, hot, steamy', with 'rust-coloured water'. When the Wasbies learned that Ma was coming to sing, they were allocated a few extra tins of food. They thought they would do well out of it and might even be able to stockpile a surplus, but they had not factored in how many extra troops would arrive to hear her. All the additional supplies were eaten up by hungry servicemen.

These included Private Tom Cattle of 2nd Battalion Dorsetshire Regiment, an apprentice butcher from the pretty Dorset village of Corfe Castle before he joined up, who had been fighting in Kohima. He describes how, after Japanese resistance diminished after 13 May:

We could now walk about without being fired on by snipers. But we were still being shelled by Jap guns being controlled by Japs on the high hills overlooking Kohima. I was filthy, unshaven, covered in impetigo, covered in lice, with boils on my arms. My feet were in a terrible condition. We were thin, hungry, thirsty and tired.

We were taken to Dimapur and had a rest. We were visited by an ENSA party including Vera Lynn. I got so thin, I was clapping so hard, off went my wedding ring and I thought I would never find it. But afterwards, with some other chaps, among the mud, I found it.

Corporal Peter Reeves was also there in Dimapur to listen to Ma sing, and he had also been fighting in Kohima, as part of the West Kent Regiment that had

199

stood firm against the Japanese in the thirteen-day siege. His daughter Sandra wrote to my mother to tell her about it.

First I must say I feel honoured that Dad has asked me to write to you with his memories of life in India and Burma. Dad joined the army on 4/3/1943 in Maidstone, Kent, the Queen's Own Royal West Kent Regiment 4th Battalion. Dad's battalion travelled by ship from Liverpool to Bombay which took 28 days, arriving early in 1944. They then all travelled by train to Deolali and then by foot to Dimapur and then fighting through the jungle to Kohima. Dad was at the siege of Kohima which lasted 13 days so we are so very lucky to have him as this was the most brutal battle in Burma and sometimes Dad told me they thought they were on their own fighting the Japanese, but with the help of Assam Regiment and the Assam Rifles they held their own and Kohima was saved. During those 13 days they had lost a lot of brave men. From there Dad's battalion travelled to Imphal and on to Burma, this is where Dad saw you. Dad has always spoken highly of you and you hold a special place in his heart. Dad said your visit brought so much joy and life back into the troops when they most needed it as they thought their country had forgotten about them. He has asked me to thank you from the bottom of his heart. Dad was under contract in the army even when the war had ended so he stayed in Burma until 1947. One of the saddest days of Dad's life was when his best friend Ronnie Jeals was killed 3

200

weeks before the end of the war in Burma. Dad still sends poppies out to Rangoon every Remembrance Day as this is where Ronnie is buried. Dad was also at the signing in Rangoon Government House on 15 August 1945 VJ Day and his uniform on that day was jungle green with a white belt. Dad finally arrived back in Liverpool on HMS Devonshire then had to make his way back to Aldershot.

There are a few things that really stand out for me from my mother's time in Dimapur, and perhaps the most vivid of them is her account of feeling so rotten in one of the many hospitals she visited there. By that time she had been to lots of hospitals and was used to being around men who were sick and wounded, but when I read about the conditions in some of the medical facilities, I am not surprised that she reacted the way she did. War, when it is as frighteningly intense as it was in Kohima, and when you get as close to it as Ma did, is a deeply unpleasant and fearful thing.

At Imphal, for instance, Len Thornton worked in the 41st Indian General Hospital's operating theatre, which he says was 'like a butcher's shop and every case needed major surgery; arms off, legs off, sometimes both; bayonet wounds, bullet wounds, horrendous burns and lots of head injuries. It went on and on, every day and every night. We never knew what to expect . . . we were all feeling the strain of this non-stop onslaught and even our instruments were wearing out.'

In his book *Burma, The Forgotten War* (John Murray, 2004), John Latimer tells the story of Sergeant

William Robinson, who was evacuated from Kohima and sent down to Dimapur on a stretcher with a leg wound. I must warn you that it is a rather gruesome little story.

> *My leg was bad by this stage, putrefying. Eventually, when I got down to the bottom the medical officer looked at it and said, 'Well you owe your life to these!' I said, 'What's that?' And I was maggoty — they'd cleaned it . . . I was most upset, the appearance of it. I didn't want it as my leg was so horrific. I thought 'If you've got to take it off, take it off — I don't want that!' That's as bad as I felt.*

In fact, although it may not sound like it, Robinson was lucky, because in many other cases infection quickly set in and amputations were common. This is why the hospital that Ma visited smelled so awful and made her feel so unwell.

Tom Cattle, who had gone down to Dimapur to see my mother sing, went back up to Kohima in the days that followed her performance, in order to clear any remaining Japanese troops from the area. His platoon clambered steeply up through thick jungle before they came under fire from enemy forces. In the darkness, they decided to stay where they were and dig in. It was hot, and as they worked, Cattle took his helmet off. At that moment, the Japanese troops opened fire again and he felt something slap him on the back of the head and knock him out. When he came round, he had blood pouring out of the back of his head. Someone bandaged him up, put him on a stretcher and carried him all the way back down the densely

202

forested slope they had just climbed up to Kohima, where there was now a dressing station. The dressing station was full of casualties. Cattle says: 'I wasn't all that bad. I had a bit of shrapnel in the back of my head. Others had lost legs, lost arms. People were shouting and screaming; such a lot of noise.' It was not over, though; just three days later, he had terrible pain in his wound and down the back of his neck. Infection had set in, and at that stage they didn't have any penicillin up in Kohima. Instead, they operated, cut out the infected flesh, and it gradually got better.

I think it is worth emphasising just how terrible the wounds and the overall circumstances were in these hospitals and dressing stations in the Kohima, Dimapur and Imphal area at this time. The fighting was of such intensity and at such close quarters that the injuries were truly horrendous. Even when faced with such appalling conditions, though, my mother was still able to show her compassion and help soldiers who were in desperate need of some comfort. This was especially the case with the two badly injured soldiers she sang for in their hospital beds — Gunner Fred Thomas and Private John Badger. This quickly became known about within the army, and I think it improved my mother's reputation even further. This letter from Private Pottrell, written soon afterwards, demonstrates what the troops thought of her gesture:

Several of my pals and I were talking the other evening about you, and one of them related an instance where you had sung in a hospital ward to two very badly wounded soldiers at Dimapur. How they were so helpless that they had to lay on

*their backs, and how you took one of them in
your arms and sang especially for him.*
[. . .]
*I am sure that those two wounded soldiers were
given new hope and a desire to get well, which
would have been lacking had it not been for your
splendid action. We who have been out here so
long, know what it is to hear the loving
tenderness of a woman's voice.*

It is difficult to imagine what it was like for the
servicemen in Burma, wounded or otherwise, with so
many compounding factors making it an incredibly
tough experience. John Latimer, writing about the
troops at Kohima, summed this up brilliantly:

*For the soldiers the constant strain was the
hardest thing to bear; severe physical pressure
under constant downpour and on pitiful rations,
with the psychological effect of constantly losing,
through one means or another, old friends with
whom one had trained and lived, sometimes for
years. The wounded knew there was little chance
of their getting right back to 'Blighty' — home.*

The scene at Kohima was apocalyptic, but by the
time my mother left Dimapur on 24 May, the men
were able to start burying the dead, who lay all
around. Lord Mountbatten described it as 'probably
one of the greatest battles in history . . . in effect the
Battle of Burma . . . naked unparalleled heroism'. But it
did come at a significant cost: during the battle,
British and Indian forces lost 4,064 men. The Japanese
casualties were 5,764.

If the Japanese had committed fewer troops to Kohima and marched a large contingent of their men on to Dimapur at the start of April, the outcome of the entire campaign could have been different, as Slim himself later admitted. A Japanese breakthrough at Dimapur would have cut off lines of communication to Stilwell's troops on the northern front. Back in April, one of the problems was that Dimapur was an administrative centre and there were actually relatively few fighting troops available to defend it from attack. When Slim had asked the brigadier commanding the town at the end of March how many actual soldiers there were amongst the 45,000 men stationed there, the brigadier replied, 'I might get five hundred who know how to fire a rifle!' The defence of Dimapur was Slim's top priority, as he saw it as being the main strategic target for the Japanese. Under threat of attack, and with the very real threat of Japanese incursion, the town pulled together, defences were dug, and preparations were made. Slim remembered reviewing Dimapur's preparedness for attack. 'As I walked round, inspecting bunkers and rifle pits, dug by non-combatant labour under the direction of storemen and clerks, and as I looked into the faces of the willing but untried garrison, I could only hope that I imparted more confidence than I felt.'

He later admitted that he had badly underestimated the Japanese capacity for large-scale long-range infiltration, but that he did understand that the most important thing was to hold Dimapur. 'The loss of Kohima we could endure,' he wrote, 'but that of Dimapur, our only base and railhead, would have been crippling to an almost fatal degree. It would have pushed into the far distance our hopes of relieving

Imphal, laid bare to the enemy the Brahmaputra Valley with its string of airfields, cut off Stilwell's Ledo Chinese, and stopped all supply to China.'

By the middle of May, after the Japanese had committed an entire division in attempting to take and hold Kohima, and failed in their mission, the threat to Dimapur itself had largely been averted. Naga village, at the northern end of the Kohima ridge, and the hills around still held some Japanese troops, and on 22 May, 2-inch and 3-inch mortars of 33 Brigade began pounding enemy positions, continuing for the next forty-eight hours. On 23 May, it rained heavily at night and into the following morning. On the 25th, the big artillery guns opened up and allowed tanks to get in position and continue to clear Japanese troops from the hillsides. For Michael Lowry, who was suffering with malaria that the monsoon rain was making even worse, this was the end of his time in Kohima; the medical officer ordered him to be evacuated soon after lunch that day. He said his goodbyes and reflected on his time at Kohima, his sadness at losing so many men and his pride in what they had achieved.

Some of the casualties were very young, perhaps barely 20, and had no chance to experience life. There were many who were in their 20s and 30s, recently married with babies and young children. The impact of those losses did not hit one at the time, but it did when the heat was off and one had time to reflect. It said so much for their loyalty, dedication and discipline that they endured and overcame the mental and physical extreme conditions of fighting a tenacious enemy.

Back down in Dimapur, my mother sang on the morning of 24 May in the torrential rain, and one report suggests that she did encore after encore. Apparently, according to a story that I have heard, the officer in charge was forced to intervene because otherwise she would have sung until she was completely exhausted. Although, from the description of the weather, it sounds like it was not the same performance that Frederick Weedman went to, his description I think gives a great idea of what it must have been like.

'C' Company 7th Worcestershire Regiment and the rest of the men of the 4th Brigade were divided in their opinion of her voice. But not after that hot steamy evening in 1944 in the Burmese jungle, when we stood in our hundreds and watched a tall, fair-haired girl walk on to a makeshift stage and stand beside an old piano.

It was Vera Lynn. She had travelled all that way with ENSA to entertain our troops in the Far East. She sang half a dozen songs in a strong clear voice. We could hear every word.

She tried to leave the stage but the men were clapping and cheering. She sang three more songs but still they went on cheering. She started to sing again but whenever she tried to stop, they yelled the name of another tune. She sang until her make-up was running in dark furrows down her cheeks, until her dress was wet with sweat, until her voice had become a croak.

She was the only ENSA star we ever saw in the jungle. There were a lot of men, that hot and humid evening, who were grateful to Vera Lynn for having remembered them so far from home and the evening of entertainment she had provided.

As one of the lads said . . . 'With a couple of weeks' training, she would make a damn good soldier.'

As the men came down from the wet hills after — and I don't think it is any exaggeration to say this — some of the hardest fighting for a generation, it must have felt miraculous to arrive in Dimapur and hear my mother sing. Many of them had tears rolling down their faces as she stood in front of them in the rain. Corporal Ted Lindsay summed up the emotion that many of the boys felt in a letter to his sister, which she forwarded on to Ma. I quoted a small part of this letter in the introduction, but I believe that it is worth quoting it in more detail here to give a true sense of just how emotionally affected many of the servicemen were:

We went mad, never have I yelled, bellowed, hollered or clapped so much before. I've always yearned to see Vera, always had that ambition and, glory be to me, here she was. I literally went mad.

Gosh, honest she's marvellous, go on please agree with me this once, we gave her an ovation, all right. You can tell, she couldn't sing for ten minutes, and she cried too.

Broken hand or not, I made it clap, hard and often too, it hurt afterwards, but it was worth it, and I would do it again too.

I saw, believe it or not, blokes crying with joy

*at seeing our own Vera, honest folks she is the
soldiers' sweetheart, she belongs to the Army; the
RAF and the Navy? No, she ain't their sweetheart,
Vera wouldn't be that way.*

My mother was used to being claimed exclusively by
the army as their 'sweetheart', but of course she was
just as happy to sing for all the services — and in
Burma she often sang for the RAF.

Although there was a great deal of grumbling in
Dimapur about the rations, compared to the diet up
in the hills it was relatively luxurious. On the front line
there would often be two meals a day of hard biscuits
and jam, with tea, and one of hard biscuits and a tin
of bully beef — finely minced corned beef set in
gelatine. In the heat, the gelatine and the fat in the
beef would turn to liquid, which meant that it could
practically be drunk from the tin! In the mind of the
average soldier, though, at least bully beef was proper
meat, whereas the soy links 'sausage' was an imposter,
masquerading as meat but delivering none of its
substance.

One story that made me chuckle was how at the
Chindit landing behind enemy lines at the landing site
called Broadway at the beginning of March 1944, there
were two code words: one to indicate failure, the other
success. The code word for failure was 'soy links'; the
word for success was 'pork sausage'. I think that tells
you all you need to know about how that dubious
culinary delicacy was regarded at the time! Nonetheless, even soy links were a boon for men who had
come close to losing their lives at Kohima. Michael
Lowry appreciated his breakfast as much, I am sure,
because it commemorated his survival as for what was

contained within it: 'The Colonel and others were pleased to see me at HQ and gave me and my batman a marvellous breakfast, almost real food, but included a soy link, which I never liked, but it soon became evident that this was quite the best sausage I had ever eaten.'

As for my mother, I don't think the food bothered her one bit; in fact I think it made her appreciate simple food even more. For her, it was temporary, though, whereas for many soldiers this was the diet they would have for months and even years. My mother for many years has eaten very little red meat, preferring fish and chicken, often with rice, and always with lots of vegetables. I think this is probably one of her secrets for a long life. She has also always been careful with water — again, a legacy from Burma, where she realised how valuable that precious resource is. As anyone who has been hot and not had access to water knows, the craving for it is one of the most intense human urges for basic survival. While reading accounts at the Imperial War Museum by soldiers who had served in Burma, I came across this tremendously descriptive piece of writing by Lance Corporal William Elliott, who served in 2nd Battalion the East Lancashire Regiment. He remembered:

the long weary marches under the pitiless sun, when the sweat from our bodies soaked through our battle-dress and dried on the surface, leaving only a white salt deposit, while from our heads it ran into our eyes, stinging and blinding, coursed down our cheeks and was licked from our lips by parched tongues, which thereby became even drier, our blistered and bleeding feet, legs stiffened by marching, so that when, after a halt, we had great difficulty getting into our stride again, our rifles and Tommy guns weighed on our shoulders and the slings bit into our flesh and our packs seemed to be boring a way into our backs until they became a living, painful part of us; climbing mile upon mile of tough torturous mountain track, pressing through deep, evil-smelling mud, passing vile, stagnant mosquito-ridden pools the stench of which sometimes overpowered us, fording swift-flowing chaungs, with the water often breast high, and then continuing our march with sodden clothes which clung to our legs and slowed us down while our boots squelched at every step until we began to wonder whether the coolness of the water on our burning feet and perspiring bodies had been worth the discomfort which inevitably followed, for the sun seemed to double its heat and our feet readily blistered. How we longed for the iced-drinks of Poona and dreamed of long copious draughts of iced beer such as we knew in Durban, or the knickerbocker glories of Bombay, only to come down to earth and sip two or three drops of tepid brackish water from our bottles, which for a short time would ease the harsh dryness of our mouths and throats — I can taste now the soap-flavoured tea we often drank when water was too scarce to allow us to rinse our cups after shaving . . .

It seemed extraordinary to me that even in the midst of the battle at Kohima, the men were still expected to shave, although at the height of the siege, when water was at a premium, I gather that some of them did grow beards without being reprimanded by their officers!

Before she left Dimapur to begin the long journey home after lunch on 24 May, Ma saw one of the rarer sights of the war up until that point: Japanese prisoners of war. Down in Imphal, a handful of Japanese soldiers had been deserting and had revealed the extent of the Japanese losses — one of their regiments, for instance, had been reduced from 3,000 men to 800. More and more pressure was being placed on the Japanese army, and Slim later got an insight into the nature of this pressure — and the fear of further desertion — when he saw an order from a senior Japanese commander in which he urged his men to consider 'death as something lighter than a feather'. The order continued: ' . . . it must be expected that the division will be almost annihilated. I have confidence in your firm courage and devotion and believe that you will do your duty, but should any delinquencies occur you have got to understand that I shall take the necessary action.'

If there was even a whiff of cowardice, let alone desertion, the punishment was death by sword. It did not happen often, and regardless of what many of the Allied soldiers thought of the Japanese troops, they almost never underestimated their bravery and tenacity. Slim recorded: 'There can be no question of the supreme courage and hardihood of the Japanese soldiers who made the attempts [to recapture Imphal]. I know of no army that could have equalled them.'

Although Japanese bravery knew no bounds, the Japanese army were being beaten back across the entire Kohima-Imphal theatre. In Kohima, the Allied forces were on the offensive and had seized control of the ridge; around Imphal, the threat had almost completely diminished; the Japanese 15th Division had been soundly trounced and was beginning to disintegrate, and Allied air superiority was now virtually unchallenged. At this precise moment in time, Slim felt confident that the rest of the war in Burma could be won.

Perhaps it was a fitting time for my mother to go. She was about to leave the prisoners of war behind; the soy links, the bully beef and the stinking hospitals; the mud, the malaria and the mortars. I've no doubt that she would have stayed had she been given the choice, but, just as when the officer stepped forward to escort her from the stage when she would have carried on giving encores in the pouring rain, I think it was best for her that she took her exit and began her epic journey home.

D-Day Landing

Vera

As well as being my last full day along the Burma front line, 24 May was also Empire Day. This was something that we used to celebrate quite a bit when I was growing up, but which after the war seemed to vanish, eventually coming to be known as Commonwealth Day. I got up at eight to pack, did two hospital shows before twelve o'clock and left Dimapur at 1.30, heading back up alongside the Dhansiri River. We stopped at Jorhat, where we stayed with the District Commissioner. My diary gives no more detail than that and I am afraid I cannot recollect anything else about that final day.

I do remember flying back to Calcutta, though — I shall never forget it, in fact. Although we were up early the following morning, we waited about all day for an aircraft to take us to Calcutta because the weather was so bad. Finally, at about six in the evening, a small plane arrived at the airfield at Jorhat. It was piloted by an American. Only a lunatic would fly in that weather, the men at the base told him, but he was determined to press on, as he wanted to meet his girlfriend in Calcutta. We were also anxious to get back, now that we'd prepared ourselves for our return journey, and so we decided to go with him. Perhaps we were lunatics too. But this was really the point when I felt that all of a sudden I couldn't wait to get home.

No one could understand how we were even thinking about joining this madman in his plane, but Len and I decided that this flight could be no worse than any other leg of the journey we had already done, and we were desperate to set off. So we took off in the darkness in pouring rain with the mad American. There were no seats in the aircraft; all we had to sit on were some tin boxes. Perched on those boxes, with an aching behind, I switched between feeling sick and dozing off, so I was never really conscious of the fact that for an hour and a half, we were completely lost in the terrible weather. We eventually got to Calcutta at a quarter to midnight, with twenty minutes of fuel left. A journey that should have taken two and a half hours had taken us about six. I felt terrible, but at least we had made it.

That first day back in Calcutta, I appreciated the luxuries of the city. Compared to being out in the remote areas along the front line, this place that had seemed so strange, exotic and unknowable to me just a few weeks before felt relatively easy and comfortable to spend time in. Also, my singing commitments had virtually come to an end and so I could do pretty much as I pleased. It gave me something of an insight into how the boys might have felt when they went into Calcutta on leave after a long spell in the jungle. My first day there, 26 May, I stayed in bed until 10.30 before going for lunch and spending some time shopping in the afternoon. After all the soy links and bully beef in the jungle, eating in restaurants made me feel like I was a child let loose in a sweet shop. I think it must have been the following day that I did one more concert in a camp just outside Calcutta. I was in a large tent and the rain was hammering down on the roof so I had to sing far more loudly than I ordinarily would. The boys cried out between the songs for their favourite numbers — and we finished with all of them singing along with me.

As well as restaurants and shopping, there was also the opportunity to swim again in Calcutta, which was a wonderful experience in the hot and humid conditions. But by this time, things like swimming and shopping, as lovely as they were, did not really match up to the idea of being at home and seeing Harry and my family. Feeling rotten in the hospital up in Dimapur may have been simply a bad moment for me, brought on by terrible sights and smells, but there was also something deep inside me that yearned for an escape to the British countryside. And although I was away from the front, there was still a long way to go in order to get there.

Dinner in Calcutta with an old friend on 27 May made my desire to return home even stronger, if that were possible. Ross Parker, the co-writer of two of my most famous songs — 'There'll Always Be an England' and 'We'll Meet Again' — was serving in the army in Calcutta at the time, and it was wonderful to see him again. It struck me as nothing less than

219

extraordinary that the author of these two songs should be sitting opposite me at that precise moment when I wanted to see England and my husband again more than anything else in the world. I recalled some of the lyrics to 'There'll Always Be an England' and I thought, 'Yes — that is where I long to be.'

While there's a country lane
Wherever there's a cottage small
Beside a field of grain
There'll always be an England

Starting out the following day from Calcutta, we did an almost identical route to the outward journey, in reverse: Nagpur — Bombay — Karachi — Cairo — Gibraltar. The first leg began at five in the morning on 28 May, setting off from Dum-Dum airport at 7 a.m. and landing in Nagpur for lunch. It was blisteringly hot — an incredible 120 degrees Fahrenheit (about 49 degrees Celsius). After lunch — and I can't imagine that I ate very much in that heat — we climbed back into the plane once more, and after another couple of hours arrived in Bombay, on the opposite side of India from Calcutta. It felt wonderful to finally be heading west!

We arrived at a lovely hotel in Bombay at around 4 p.m., and I had a good rest after another long day of travelling. In the evening, we had dinner with Colonel Eric Dunstan, the ENSA man in Bombay, who we had met on the way out, and who was keen to know all about how the past few weeks had been for us. He also

220

wanted us to encourage other entertainers back in Britain to go out to India and Burma to entertain the troops. It was something he put in writing to us as well, in a note we received just before we left.

Dear Vera and Len,
I cannot tell you how much I appreciate what you have done for ENSA out here — so quickly, so effectively, so uncomplainingly, so perfectly. I thank you both with my real appreciation and gratitude.
Be good ambassadors for us at home and tell them all how much we need them out here and how we try to do our best for them when they come.
Bon voyage to you both and I hope you'll find your families safe and well at home.
Yours very sincerely,
Eric Dunstan

Before we flew on to Karachi, we had a full day in Bombay, which I spent swimming and relaxing. I even had a bath in the evening, and at dinner got news that transport would be ready in the morning to take us on the next leg of our journey. I was in bed by 9.30 and the following morning left in a Lockheed Hudson aircraft. That afternoon, I saw Stainless Stephen in Karachi. He had also been touring around India and I knew him from home. He was a unique comedian who used to sound out all the punctuation in his sentences — saying things like 'This is Stainless Aimless Stephen, semi-colon, soliloquising to oneself, semi-quaver, as is his custom.' His real name was Arthur Baynes and he was originally from Sheffield, which is where he got his name from — because of the stainless-steel industry there. He was a lot older than me — I suppose he must have been in his fifties in 1944 — but he was good company and we had a fun afternoon shopping together in Karachi.

It was there that I gave my final concerts of the tour. The first of these was on 31 May, to 2,500 of the boys who had gathered on the tennis courts. It was a great concert and I thought it would be my last — a fitting end to what felt by now a long but successful tour. However, it was soon apparent that I would not be flying home the following day, or even the day after. There were various delays while we waited for onward transport, and for the first time on the trip — I suppose because by now I was both physically exhausted and anxious to be home — I became irritated. On 1 June, I wrote in my diary that I was 'very annoyed'. However, I was able to head down to the glorious sandy beach at Manora, which had a Hindu temple behind it, and this helped improve my mood — temporarily. The following day, I was 'fed up to death'!

Rather than just hanging around waiting for a flight, I decided to do another show at RAF Drigh Road — with Stainless Stephen. After I got home, I received a kind letter about this performance, from a lady called Margaret Armstrong, from South Shields in County Durham:

On behalf of my son serving with the RAF in India, I would like to thank you for the pleasure you gave and the breath of home, when you entertained the troops. My son wrote some weeks ago and told me of the unexpected pleasure they had, when Vera Lynn and Stainless Stephen gave them a grand concert, especially as it was at the end of a Burma front tour and you were bound to be very tired. You had a few hours to spare at Karachi, and it was a grand gesture to give another concert. My son was one of the eight picked from his company and he thoroughly enjoyed the show, even if it did make him homesick.

On 3 June we finally began to head westwards again, with some kind of feeling that something was happening ahead of us. We first went to Bahrain in a flying boat, and then at 3.30 the following morning continued on to Cairo, arriving there at lunchtime on 4 June. I had hoped that we could carry straight on home, but someone called Corporal Smith told me that we would have to stay in Cairo for the night before continuing our journey. I recorded in my diary that I was 'very annoyed' again! All this might make me sound like I was rather impatient, but you have to remember that I did not yet know anything about D-Day and, with no more performances to be done, all I wanted was to be at home.

The following day we left Cairo, and I remember that the pilot took us down low over the desert so that we could see where the famous battle of El Alamein had been fought in 1942. The next stop was Djerba — a small island off Tunisia. Here, strange though it may seem now (surely it should have been a top-level secret?), I found out that the following day, 6 June, would be D-Day. So it was on D-Day that we left for Gibraltar, where I bought bananas to take home. The skies over Europe were full of planes, and I think it must have been something of a miracle that we were allowed to fly in on that most crucial of days on which all our hearts were in our mouths. Everyone had known that the invasion of Europe would happen at some point; now it was finally taking place. We were all nervous — nervous to know whether the Allies would sweep into France, or whether, like in Italy earlier in the year, we would be held up for months on the beaches.

Returning to England, I thought in those first few hours a great deal about D-Day but I also felt exhausted, emotionally flat and, I suppose, over-stimulated from the past few months. I had a feeling that I think many other people also have after a life-changing experience — a feeling that that experience could never be surpassed. But I also felt an underlying sense of contentment. I had survived. I was home. I had done what I had set out to do. Yes, I felt a little bit proud that I had done my bit and boosted the morale of the thousands of troops that I had sung for over the past few months. But most importantly, England was still here, waiting for me, and so was my faithful Harry.

Ginny

Jorhat, where Ma went from Dimapur on 24 May, was effectively the gateway to the American and Chinese divisions who were responsible for taking the fight to the Japanese on the northernmost part of the Indo-Burmese border. And it was at the airfield at Jorhat, where my mother flew from the following day, that General 'Vinegar' Joe Stilwell and General Slim had had a crucial conference at the beginning of April. Slim reported from that meeting that there was a gloomy atmosphere amongst the American airmen based in Jorhat, which he attributed mainly to the fact that they feared a ground attack. Following the adage that people fear most what they cannot control, it is no surprise that airmen worried more about attacks from the ground, and soldiers worried more about threats from the air. 'They seemed to have an idea that Japanese hordes might appear on the edge of the strip at any moment, and, knowing I had refused requests for troops to defend the American airfields . . . 'the Limey general' was not overly popular.'

By the time Ma flew out of Jorhat, the American airmen would have been far more confident that they would not be imminently attacked. There was already a sense at this point that the momentum of the entire conflict was shifting. I personally think that this is the most extraordinary thing about the whole story of my mother being out there. Her time there coincided exactly with the point at which fortunes shifted. Just six weeks earlier at the same airfield from which she was flying out, men were in fear of their lives. On 25 May, they were beginning to imagine what a victory against Japan in South East Asia might look like. Of course, I don't think it is possible for my mother to claim responsibility for the change in the fortunes of the Allies in Burma, but I do think that her presence was a small part of the overall strategy to improve the condition of the soldiers. There is no doubt that she boosted their morale, gave them something to hope for and to fight for. And I don't think the value of this can be underestimated.

My mother's flight south to Calcutta was in dark and wet conditions and it sounds like she almost did not make it. She may not have been able to look down on the jungle below her and think poetic thoughts about her time along the front line, but when I was at the Imperial War Museum, I found this fantastic account of someone who did. William Elliott, from 2nd Battalion the East Lancashire Regiment, who I quoted earlier in the book, writing about the hardships of the soldier's life in Burma, had mixed feelings as he gazed at the forested hillsides below him. I think it is a magnificent piece of writing, which touches on the fact that the soldiers did not just encounter an enemy force in Burma; they also came face to face with an often awe-inspiring natural environment that very few of them had seen before.

My last view of Burma was from a height of several thousand feet, looking down on mile after mile of dense forest, mighty ranges of hills and mountains, the panorama presented was of majestic beauty and grandeur, that even after having lived so long amongst these vast tracts of mountain and forest with their hidden pathways and rocky, winding mountain tracks, from the air they still appeared shrouded in mystery — gloomy and awe-inspiring, yet fascinating in their immensity, only the unimaginative could gaze and feel no small measure of awe or experience not one small tinge of regret as this great country which had been our home through these arduous days, receded further and further from our sight, leaving only in our minds the events which had occupied us during our sojourn there. I remembered those who had come out with us full of life and the spirit of adventure, who now for ever rested in the soil of this land, this same soil remained, in spite of the devastation of battle, almost untouched, and in a little while the scars which blemished the land would be healed by the unceasing process of nature, and the ravages of man would be forgotten, the great forests would sleep once more in deep silence, a silence enhanced rather than broken, by the song of birds, the chattering of the monkey, the cry of the leopard, the rustle of the snake, the buzz of the insects, or the trumpeting of the elusive elephant, and lulled by the ripple of the leisurely stream in its meandering to the mighty Irrawaddy or the broad Sittang.

Calcutta was the main centre for servicemen on leave from Burma, and it was different for my mother visiting it this time, after she too had been out in the wilderness for some time. I think this gave her a real

227

insight into the soldier's life and what it must have felt like for them when they came out from a combat situation and into a city. Thomas Nutt, who had heard my mother sing in Agartala a few weeks earlier, described what it meant for the men to go on leave in Calcutta.

Our only relief and relaxation at this period was an occasional weekend in Calcutta. It is a beautiful city — broad streets, palaces, memorials, a university, two railway stations, a port and an airport. It had a teeming population of two and a half million and it seemed that they were all in the city centre at one time. It was impossible to see the city for the people. While the climate from the end of November to March is very pleasant — the monsoon season from July to October brought high temperatures and unbearable humidity. Many businessmen's families left the city at this time to live in the hill stations.

But for the poor, many were left to live literally on the pavements and as the temperature rose so did the number of deaths on the street. The local newspaper, the Calcutta Statesman, *always gave the temperature and the number of corpses picked up daily. Usually the figure was similar — 95 degrees Fahrenheit, ninety to one hundred corpses.*

Despite the heat the highlight of our day was a visit to a café called Firpos in the main street Chowringee. It was always full of British servicemen on leave. Here we could get a splendid meal very cheaply. I usually had a mixed grill. I think without this occasional break we would all have gone mad. A number of the older married men did have nervous breakdowns. Some of these men had received letters telling them their wives were having an affair — they were mostly with American soldiers. This on top of the heat, the rain and the thunder — which started every afternoon in the monsoon season — was just too much for many men and it was too easy to lose control. Some were taken off to 'Dulalli', where there was a mental hospital.

It's hardly surprising that some of the men lost control — they had been under such intense pressure — but as I understand it this happened very infrequently. However, Calcutta itself was something of a pressure cooker of a different sort — politically, the city at the centre of the growing Indian nationalist movement, which gained further momentum as the war looked as though it might soon end. My mother mentions Empire Day, which fell on 24 May, but the days of the empire were coming to an end.

Mahatma Gandhi had founded the Quit India movement in 1942, after many years of activism. The movement demanded an end to British rule of India. Although it was started in Bombay, Calcutta was undoubtedly at the very centre of the movement, and the proximity of the city to the British defeats in Burma at that point poured fuel on the nationalist fire there in a number of ways. For one thing, it showed that the British could be beaten, and as tens of thousands of Indians and Britons fled from Burma, Gandhi roused outrage by pointing out the fact that white civilians had been given preferential treatment compared to native Indians. As British and Indian troops headed west in the monsoon season of 1942, away from the advancing Japanese, they were accompanied by 140,000 civilian refugees, many of whom died as they trekked by foot through the treacherous malarial jungle on the border of Burma and East Bengal.

The situation turned many in Calcutta away from an essentially apathetic attitude towards the British Raj to one of aggressive intolerance. Many soldiers got into animated, though essentially friendly, conversations with local people in Calcutta about the merits of whether India should become independent. You have to remember that many British soldiers served alongside Indians in Burma and may have had more sympathy with their nationalist sentiment than you might think. James Holland, in his book *Burma '44*, tells the story of Trooper Tom Grounds of the 25th Dragoons, who at a coffee house in Calcutta heard an Indian quote Sir Walter Scott: 'Breathes there the man with soul so dead, who never to himself hath said: 'This is my own, my native land!' . . . ' Grounds found it difficult to argue with this, but he felt, most importantly, 'that the Japs had to be defeated first'. One of the great tragedies that would befall some of the Indian troops who fought the Japanese in Burma was that they ended up fighting against their own comrades during partition, Hindus against Muslims. But that is a story for a different book.

It was an amazing coincidence that Ross Parker, who co-wrote two of Ma's most famous songs, should have been in Calcutta at the same time as her, and I think she loved having the opportunity to meet a familiar face who had been so instrumental in her success. Those two songs — 'We'll Meet Again' and

'There'll Always Be an England' — summed up absolutely how Ma was feeling at that moment in time. It is just one of a number of things that suggested to me that there was something fateful about the whole adventure and made me want to write about it: the fact that everything fell into place so perfectly, that she survived this epic experience unscathed; the fact that so many different coincidences happened; and the fact that Ma, while never being anything other than her genuine self, was to so many thousands of men a shining beacon of hope. In a way it is an ordinary story about a singer going to entertain the troops, but it is the accumulation of these details that to me make it seem extraordinary.

Leslie Munder was among the audience for Ma's final performance in Calcutta. He remembered:

It was in the middle of the wet season and rained every day very heavy indeed. After a few days we were told 'You lucky lads are going to have Vera Lynn to sing to you.' That pleased us no end. We all love Vera. We then proceed to some tent a few yards away. There was only tents in this camp. Just to hold us a few days before travelling to places in India to regroup.

There was Vera with a few companions. No music. Vera was standing under the eaves of a tent in the pouring rain. Vera sang loud so that she could be heard above the sound of the heavy rain. We all joined a grand singsong. We thought what a wonderful lady to stand there in the heavy rain and sing to us, we gave her a wonderful cheer. She waved and went to sing somewhere else.

231

It is to be remembered that whilst at Kohima and Calcutta Vera was lucky not to get malaria or dysentery. So many died of these illnesses.

You may remember a man called Major Jack Bontemps, the ENSA representative in Calcutta, who kindly lent Ma his bungalow when she could not sleep in a room above the laundry. At the same time as my mother left India, Bontemps wrote this note.

My Dear Vera & Len,
By the time you receive this I trust you will be safe and sound in England and that you had a reasonable and comfortable journey home.
[. . .]
Now that you are away from India I personally thank you ever so much for the wonderful work you have performed out here. Believe me from reports received in this office I can assure you the boys do thank you from the bottom of their hearts.

On the other hand I would also like to thank you for roughing it the way you did while you were out here.

You both already know that I did not set myself out to fuss over you and I am sure you will be the first to appreciate this. When I do return to London I shall make sure that I contact you and perhaps then as a civilian I may be able to tell you all I really think.

Before she left India, though, there were a couple more days in Bombay, which was also the place where servicemen who had fought in Burma would make their way home from. They would go by ship, rather than flying as my mother did, usually via Durban in South Africa. This was the route taken by Arthur Webberley and his mate Ern Mellet (who, if you remember, used sneaky tactics to get my mother's autograph at Bawli Bazar, in the Arakan), where they continued to stretch the rules!

We returned to Bombay at the end of our engagement, sailing home on the Dorset *troop-ship. On this journey Ern and I were on the baggage security and we discovered a sack of candied peel (the real thing). Both rather partial to this delicacy we paid daily trips to the hold, shrinking the sack somewhat.*

The journey by boat would take a month, whereas Ma's journey would take just a few days, beginning by flying to Karachi, which in those pre-partition days was still in India. One thing that struck me about Ma's trip to Karachi is that her penultimate concert took

233

place on the tennis courts there. She may not have known it at that moment, but back in Burma, the tennis court at Kohima (when you think about it, such a tiny piece of ground) had been the site of one of the bloodiest parts of the battle. It had been completely destroyed by ordnance and literally hundreds of men had lost their lives on it. There is something horribly surreal about a pitched battle being fought on the site of that most genteel of British sports.

Fergal Keane, in his book *Road of Bones: The Epic Siege of Kohima 1944*, tells the story of Lance Corporal Dennis Wykes of the West Kents. Wykes was dug in at the tennis court in the second week of April and described the awful attacks that were launched from the terrace just below the other end of the court, little more than twenty yards away. 'They came howling and screaming and full of go. It was terrifying but the only good thing was the screaming let you know where they were coming from and so we got our lines of fire right and mowed them down. Wave after wave we cut them down with machine guns.' It just strikes me as another of those little coincidences on Ma's tour, something that, looking back at it, adds to the poignancy of her time there: a tennis court could be a site of horrendous slaughter, but it could also be a place to be enchanted by music and be reminded of home.

I am not surprised that my mother felt anxious to return home and a little frustrated that aircraft were not available to transport her there. She cannot have known it at the time, but with D-Day taking place so imminently, and so many aircraft in the skies over Europe, the logistics must have been incredibly complex. I am certain, too, that the men in the RAF responsible for getting her home wanted to make sure, above all else, that she was safe. If that meant a delay in her schedule, then that was a small price to pay. It seems strange to me that she heard rumours about D-Day, which quickly became substantiated, on her journey home in the days before the invasion — surely this was one of the best-kept secrets of the war so far? But I suppose that many people had to know about it, and if there was one person they felt they could trust, it was Vera Lynn!

But what a momentous day to land back in England. In Burma, the tide had turned; coming back to Europe, Ma found that the Allies were also taking a crucial step closer to winning the war against the Nazis. I'm not surprised that one of her biggest fears at that point was that her life might feel like a bit of an anticlimax from then on.

We'll Meet Again

Vera

I remember seeing a press story from June 1944, immediately after I got back from Burma, that said something like: 'Vera Lynn is back from the Burma battlefront after entertaining the troops there, looking well but tired.' The papers may often be guilty of exaggeration, but in this instance 'tired' wouldn't even begin to cover it. The fact was that I was completely exhausted and felt that I would never be able to sleep for long enough to make up for it. When I looked back on it later in life, I realised that my fatigue was brought on by many different things. Of course there was the endless travelling, which had included as many flights in a few months as I would probably make in the whole of the following decade; and plenty of long journeys down bumpy, unforgiving tracks, through dust and mud and jungle. Then there was all the singing. Quite often, I was doing at least two proper shows in a day as well as impromptu singalongs in various hospitals, messes and tents. Combined with this was the heat, humidity, thunderous monsoon rain and biting insects.

But what I don't think I thought about then was the mental strain of all of this, and the fact that I had almost no time to myself — when I wasn't performing or travelling, I was signing autographs or having lunch or dinner with the boys, or speaking to patients in the hospital, or meeting army and RAF bigwigs. It was very seldom that I was able to just sit down and be on my own. I also think, looking back, that some of the more terrible things that I saw — badly wounded and sick men, some of whom I know did not make it — probably affected me more than I understood at the time. That was all part of keeping a stiff upper lip, of carrying on, even though I may not always have wanted to. That's just what people did then. That is how we won the war.

Of course I have never forgotten — and I felt it at the time — that I was one of the luckiest ones; I was suffering from nothing more than exhaustion, nobody close to me had been killed in the war, and I was fortunate enough to be able to take some time off. I felt more than anything at that moment that I needed a spell in the country, away from London; indeed, away from everyone and everything apart from Harry. I did sing on the radio very soon after I got back, but almost immediately after that, Harry and I spent a couple of weeks in Mrs Higlet's little semi-detached country cottage in Weybourne, near Farnham. When I was in the hospital in Dimapur, this was where I had dreamed of being, and the peace and quiet of the countryside helped me to recover.

The cottage wasn't linked up to the mains, so we had no electricity, water or gas: nothing. And it was all the better for it. I had become accustomed to a simple life in Burma, and I had returned without craving luxury — not that there was a great deal of it around in England in 1944! The simple food out in Burma had not been a problem for me, and I continued to have a simple life back home. Behind the cottage there was an outdoor toilet — or privy — and an acre of garden, where they grew all their own vegetables. And of course there was Annie Walker's well — the same well I had dreamed of in Burma, with water so clean and cool.

In Weybourne I immediately felt better, and I knew within a few days of being there that once my health was fully restored, I would be back singing and touring again. It did not take that long — within a few weeks I felt fully myself again. I was back doing all those things I had done before I went to Burma, and life, as much as it could during wartime, returned to normal. 'Normal' in wartime, though, meant all kinds of things that we might think extraordinary in peacetime. That summer, for instance, the house we had been renting in Upney Lane, Barking, was damaged when a landmine fell in the next street. The explosion made the upper floor of the house uninhabitable, and so we spent much our time in the cellar, with the furniture from the top storey crammed down there with us! It was not a way of life that we wanted to continue with for too much longer, and after enjoying spending time in the cottage so much, I was keen to think about moving to the countryside.

It so happened that in August, I was doing a week at the Brighton Hippodrome and Harry was with me. If you remember, Brighton was where Harry had said to me in 1939, for the umpteenth time, 'I'm going to marry you.' And rather than laugh at him, or pretend I hadn't heard, I had said, 'Yes, you are.' So perhaps that had something to do with what happened next as well. We decided to take a look at houses nearby; perhaps there was a cottage we could rent, or at the very least, a place where we could move our furniture while we got everything sorted in London. Instead, we ended up buying a twenty-two-room house called Clayton Holt, which came with 198 acres of land!

Clayton Holt was more than a house — much more: it offered us a chance of a new way of life, and to start a family. I was twenty-seven, I'd already had a wonderful singing career; now I wanted children. Harry had been suffering from painful nasal polyps and was struggling to play his instrument. He left the RAF band and in many ways the future seemed unpredictable for him. We thought that the land, with a seven-acre orchard and 1,100 fruit trees, might provide him with a new career as a market gardener as well as the healthy outdoor lifestyle that was recommended by his doctor.

That summer and autumn, it felt like the end of the war might not be too far away. I took a much closer interest in what was happening in Burma than I had previously, and saw with some satisfaction that the defeats the Fourteenth Army had inflicted upon the Japanese at Imphal and Kohima had completely turned the tide. Now the boys I had sung for out there were chasing the Japanese army back east, through the heart of Burma. In Europe, the Battle of Normandy that summer was a tough, hard-fought campaign, but by the end of August, the Germans were also in headlong retreat out of France. The RAF had all but crushed the German bombers, but that summer, soon after I got back, there was a new threat from the skies — V-1 flying bombs, or doodlebugs as we called them. Then, in September, they started sending over V-2 rockets, which were enormous and terrifying. I remember that the first one hit Chiswick in west London at the start of September. One of the chaps from Burma wrote to me after I got back to say that 'Out here we follow the European war with great interest and grieve to think of the hardship Southern England has gone through these last few months with flying bombs, V-2 etc. Hope none come your way.'

This was not a great time and people were scared — of course they were. But there were also a lot of jokes. 'It was all quiet until you came home,' some people laughingly told me (the V-1S started coming over the week after I got back!). We'd been through the Blitz and survived the worst they could throw at us. Londoners were tired, but there was also a different attitude to life. You knew that you could get killed in London — most of us knew people who had been — so it didn't seem to be any more dangerous being in Burma that it was back in Britain. What was the difference between being killed by Japanese artillery or malaria in the jungle and a V-2 rocket in London? The flying bombs served as a reminder why the decision to

243

go to the Far East had not really been such a dramatic one.

I already felt at that point that I had been lucky with my career, and I thought as the war came to an end that my success might end with it. I had been in the music business long enough to know that it is as full of fads and fashions as anything else. So, without making any formal announcement, I devoted the next couple of years of my life to having a family. My daughter Virginia, who has helped me write this book, was born in 1946, and I didn't perform again until 1947; even then it was only largely because I still had a contract to fulfil. I felt, though, that the public still appreciated me, and as I am sure every performer would tell you, there is nothing like the sound of warm applause and cheers.

In the early 1950s, I continued to have success as a recording artist, with a number of hits such as 'Forget Me Not', and 'Auf Wiederseh'n Sweetheart', in which I was accompanied by men from all three of the services. I even had a lot of success in America at this time and spent quite a bit of time in New York, where I regularly appeared on Tallulah Bankhead's radio programme *The Big Show*. During the war I had been a regular in the West End, and I remained very close to the variety entertainment world. In the early 1950s I was fortunate to star alongside two of the decade's most famous and talented comedians — Jimmy Edwards and Anthony Hancock — in a comedy revue called *London Laughs* at the Adelphi Theatre on the Strand. It was an enormous success and ran for two years.

I even had my own variety show on television in the sixties and seventies and I was a guest on a number of other shows of that type, most memorably with Morecambe and Wise in 1972. I mention all of this not because I want to tell you the whole of the rest of my life story — after all, I wrote my autobiography some years ago — but because I think it is important to put my Burma trip into some context. I had a busy, active life in the decades after the war and sang in public all the way up to the fiftieth anniversary of VE Day, in 1995. Yet despite all of that, the journey to Burma is etched in my brain, full of all sorts of intense memories. On reflection, I think that in some ways I never quite got over that period of my life. My memories of the wartime years are certainly strongest when I think of Burma. And I find it difficult to imagine the young woman I was then. It was a strange and wonderful experience that has lived with me for the rest of my life. It was important to me at the time and still is now: I feel privileged to have done it and I have always carried with me the memory of all the brave men I met who were fighting that 'forgotten' war that made such a difference to our freedom.

I was able to meet some of those men again at various reunions after the war. I felt connected to them at those events — I was not just someone going to sing a few songs; I felt that I was one of them. I still do. Back in 1985, they awarded me the War Medal and the Burma Star, which was a very proud moment for me. And in 2004, I went to a sixtieth anniversary reunion for Burma veterans at London's Imperial War Museum. It was the anniversary not just of my visit to Burma, but also of those decisive battles at Imphal, Kohima and Ngakyedauk fought by the Fourteenth Army in the vicious Burma jungle campaign, which turned the conflict in our favour.

More than a hundred veterans attended, many in their eighties and nineties. To my astonishment, there was one man there who looked familiar. You may remember Major Neville Hogan, the soldier in the Chindit long-range penetration brigade who I met briefly in Dibrugarh, in the north of the Indo-Burmese border. When I visited him in hospital back then, he asked me for a kiss. At the reunion, he reminded me of that occasion sixty years ago and, with a glint in his eye, suggested that we do it once more. I agreed. I held his hand and kissed him on the forehead, and he kissed me on the cheek.

Ginny

My mother's arrival home on D-Day is another of those resonating historical coincidences about her journey — like the fact that her visit to Burma took place during those decisive battles at Kohima and Imphal — and it is also a convenient bookend to this story. I think that D-Day probably allowed her to 'pass under the radar' as she returned home, because the focus of the entire country was on what was happening on the beaches of Normandy. This, I am sure, suited her — at that moment in time I get the impression that she wanted to vanish for a little bit, to spend time in the country with Daddy and be away from everyone else. Her exhaustion was certainly profound and it took her quite a few weeks to fully recover from it. My theory about that is that it was as much about emotional exhaustion as physical tiredness. I don't think that before she left for Burma Ma could possibly have understood the depth of feeling and raw emotion that she would come across there. The men responded to her visit with an outpouring of emotion that rather goes against that idea of the stiff upper lip. Many men — of course not all, but certainly a large number — openly cried at her performances.

Corporal Ted Lindsay, who had recounted in a letter to his sister in 1944 witnessing, 'believe it or not, blokes crying with joy at seeing our own Vera', also wrote that my mother was deeply affected by the outpouring of emotion, when he describes how 'we gave her an ovation, all right. You can tell, she couldn't sing for ten minutes, and she cried too.' Signalman H. Jackson of the 17th India Division Signals was not able to hear Ma sing in Burma, but related to her in a letter how when he and his comrades returned from the front line, they managed to get hold of a 'wireless given to us on our first night free from war'. The first thing they heard when they turned it on was my mother singing.

This strikes at the very heart of why my mother became so successful during the war, but for me it also shows why the trip was so exhausting for her. She gave all the men she sang for an emotional outlet; for the soldiers and airmen in Burma, who felt so isolated and far away from home, the emotions were amplified and she became their connection with home. My mother may not agree, but I feel that by serving as this emotional connection, by representing their hopes and dreams, by linking the men to their wives, families and sweethearts, she became emotionally exhausted. They invested so much in her, and she tried to give everything she could back to them. Of course I would say this — I am her daughter after all — but I think there was something heroically selfless about her complete openness and willingness to engage emotionally with the soldiers in this way. Mrs Luckford, the sister of a soldier in the Royal Artillery in Burma, sent a letter soon after Ma had got home, with some lines she had copied from her brother's letter. I think it sums this point up rather well.

I have just heard Vera Lynn sing again. Whatever anyone says about her singing, it goes down well *out here. I assure you, up in the forward areas where she is, she has done bloody marvels for the troops. It is literally true that the men <u>love her</u>; not as a sweetheart, but she acts off the stage more as a sister. She really is sincere in all she does. She comes from the same class as most of the men and to give an example of how she goes about off the stage I'll tell you what she has done here. After giving shows, in the morning, afternoon and evening every conceivable place, she will not go and have meals with brigadiers and generals who offer her some, but she goes off to the chaps' messes and canteens and chats, eats and sings to them. One day she visited a hospital and actually talked to about 2,000 patients — poor girl, she must have been weary. She is the most unaffected star I've ever met. I'm afraid a girl like this makes us a little homesick, but it does one's heart good to hear her sing and talk with her — the first woman of ENSA to come to the jungle — God bless her.*

After my mother left the jungle and rice paddies of Burma, it became clear that the Allies had seized the upper hand, not just in Kohima and Imphal, but across the entire theatre. Around the same time as her arrival back in Britain, though, Slim was struck down by malaria, something that annoyed him in two ways — firstly because this was a particularly interesting and important moment in the war as a whole, and secondly because he had always stated that getting malaria was a breach of discipline. He had in fact not followed his own orders and bathed after sunset one evening, when he had been bitten by mosquitoes. I

249

am sure he gave himself a stern talking-to as he lay in hospital in Shillong, following all the key movements on the battlefield from his bed.

The heavy monsoon rains were slowing everything down, but there was no doubt in which direction things were going. By the middle of June, even the famed Japanese 31st Division was falling apart, and the Fourteenth Army was keen to press home its advantage. Slim's tactic of letting the Japanese advance to a place where they could be heavily defeated had been effective; now it was a case of capitalising on the Japanese volte-face and advancing before they had an opportunity to regroup and potentially counterattack. So began a period of the war that Slim would later call the 'pursuit' — chasing the Japanese army relentlessly and at speed deeper and deeper into the Burmese jungle. The momentum was with the Allied troops in many different ways: they were gaining superiority in terms of territory; they were now a better fighting force in the conditions that they had previously found so intimidating; and, perhaps most importantly, they had the psychological edge. They no longer believed that Japanese soldiers were invincible; many in the Fourteenth Army now felt in their hearts, for the first time, that they were the stronger force — better trained, better adapted to the jungle, unafraid and fierce — and that they were going to win this terrible war that they were fighting. It is a great credit to Slim that in the space of a few months he had played a major role in transforming a largely demoralised, disease-ridden and under-trained force into one of the most intimidating collections of soldiers he could ever have dreamed of commanding.

The Japanese pulled back. At first they hoped to

hold the area between the Chindwin and Irrawaddy rivers. But then they retreated still further, to the east of the Irrawaddy. As the Allied troops advanced, the terrible sights of war encouraged them: abandoned guns and tanks, and the bodies of enemy soldiers scattered among them. Even in flight, though, the Japanese proved to be a remarkably dogged and determined enemy. Slim noted that only one prisoner would be taken for every hundred enemy soldiers that were killed — a number far smaller than with any other army. For the Japanese it must have been a terrible time, being hounded and harangued as they retreated through the mud and the misery of the monsoon.

The main Fourteenth Army offensive began after the monsoon rains had finished, and from December 1944 through to the middle of February 1945 there was fierce fighting to the west of the Irrawaddy as the Japanese tried to keep the Allied forces at bay. But their efforts were in vain: the Fourteenth Army crossed the Irrawaddy and the town of Meiktila fell on 5 March. The Japanese fought back and tried to retake the town with desperate suicide attacks, but by the end of March their resistance had been completely crushed. Mandalay, right in the centre of Burma, was captured a couple of weeks later, and the race was then on to get to Rangoon before the monsoon season came once more. The army advanced at speed, covering twenty, thirty, even forty miles in a day. By the beginning of May, they had arrived at Rangoon; on 1 May, a battalion of the 50th Indian Parachute Regiment dropped at Elephant Point (the same place Ma had mistakenly written in her diary that she'd visited the year before).

There was little opposition to the Allied forces entering the city, and thousands of the inhabitants came out onto the streets to welcome the victors. Just a week later it was VE Day — the war in Europe was over. But in Burma, there were scattered remnants of Japanese troops in many different locations and they continued to fight on. It wasn't until the beginning of August that the last Japanese resistance in Burma came to an end and the war was finally over.

While my mother had been away in Burma, the war in Europe had also moved forward in giant strides. In particular, the Soviet Union had advanced all along the eastern front, to take strategic cities including Yalta, Odessa and Sebastapol on the Black Sea in the south, all the way up to the territory around Leningrad on the Baltic Sea in the north. Before D-Day, the other main theatre of operation had been in Italy, where on 14 May, at the fourth attempt, the crucial breakthrough was finally made at Monte Cassino. Nine days later, while Ma was in Dimapur, the Allies launched their breakout from the Anzio perimeter. Since January, tens of thousands of British and American troops had been trapped on the beachhead by German forces under the leadership of Field Marshal Kesselring. The defence mounted by the Germans was both masterful and stubborn, but on the morning of 23 May, the Allied big guns bombarded German positions, before air support joined in the action. Then infantry and tanks moved forward to breach the German defences. The breakthrough was another significant chapter in the war in Europe. Just twelve days later, on 4 June, Rome was liberated, though that also meant that the Allies missed an important opportunity to destroy the German Tenth

Army, a mistake that would haunt them for many months to come.

At home, despite the generally positive news from Europe and the Far East, morale was not high. A Ministry of Information report in the spring of 1944 described domestic morale as 'poor', and there were strikes in various parts of the country, from Wales to Yorkshire, as disaffection spread. One of the great worries of the time was how costly an invasion of Europe would be in terms of the number of lives lost. More than anything, though, I think people were tired. Tired of the war; tired of worrying; tired of being separated from their loved ones and not knowing when they might see them again. Behind the scenes, the government knew that Hitler would soon be launching new secret weapons — the V-1 and V-2 flying bombs — and there was, understandably, concern at the highest levels about whether D-Day and Operation Overlord would be successful. Sir Frederick Morgan, who was involved in planning D-Day, later declared that 'Until the invasion of NW Europe was actually demonstrated to be successful, I believe [the prime minister] had the conviction it could not succeed.'

D-Day was the start of the bigger Operation Overlord — the campaign to liberate north-west Europe from German occupation. It began with 24,000 American, British and Canadian airborne forces parachuting into northern France very early on the morning of 6 June, and was followed by the largest seaborne invasion in history as the initial wave of 100,000 ground troops landed on five beaches, codenamed Utah, Omaha, Gold, Juno and Sword. Intense fighting followed as the Allies tried to gain a

253

foothold in Normandy, the invading forces battling up beaches scoured with machine-gun and artillery fire, through barbed wire, minefields, smoke and flame. By the end of that day, though, they had established bases a few miles inland and secured a chain of positions that would ultimately link together. All the time, hundreds of thousands more troops poured on to the beaches. The operation was a great success, and by 12 June, Churchill was even able to visit Normandy. There was a long fight ahead, but the foundations had been established that would eventually lead the Allies to Berlin and the toppling of Hitler's Third Reich.

It seems clear from a number of letters written to Ma on 13 June, welcoming her home from Burma, that she was on the radio the same day as Churchill visited the Normandy coast, singing some of the songs that the boys had requested on her tour. 'Yesterday I heard you sing on the radio and mention the 'boys' you left in Burma, Bengal and Assam,' reads one of them. 'Welcome Home!' wrote Edna Bateman from Cumberland. 'It's simply grand to have you back home again, safe and sound. I know you must be tired out but you have done a grand job and I know our loved ones out in India will appreciate your visit very much.'

Mrs R. Hackford of Whitwick, near Leicester, also sent her thanks:

I have a brother in the Indian Command and he wrote and told me he had just come back to India from the Burmese jungle and who do you think, Dear Sister, was there to greet us but Vera Lynn in person. What a grand tonic for the troops those were his own words. I am thankful that you have

254

been spared to come back to dear old England once more.

A Mrs House wrote on 12 June:

I hope you will forgive me writing to you, but I have just heard your first broadcast since you came back from India, and I want to say 'thank you very much' for going out there to brighten the lives of the men who are so very far from home. My only son who is in Burma wrote and told me all about your visit, he was just recovering from a glider crash and he said how very much the boys enjoyed your songs. He said you signed lots of autographs and I hope he was lucky enough to get one too. I shall look forward to hearing you again soon, and I have written to him to say you sang the song they asked you to. So thanking you once again.

Similarly, Edna Smith from Bath wrote to thank Ma for performing for her husband. 'I want to thank you very much indeed for all the pleasure you gave to my husband and all the men with him when you visited their camp in India,' she wrote. 'I know how very much they appreciated it.'

But on 13 June, a new threat came to London and the south-east of England in the form of the V-1 flying bomb, or doodlebug. The following Sunday, a V-1 killed 121 people amongst a mixed congregation of civilians and servicemen at a service in the Guards' Chapel at Wellington Barracks on Birdcage Walk, not far from Buckingham Palace. I think my mother was out in the countryside by this stage, but even there, the threat from V-1s was very real, as they peppered the entire south-east of England that summer. The public mood had certainly been improved by military successes like D-Day, the liberation of Rome, and Slim's victories against the Japanese at Kohima and Imphal, but it was also dented by fear of Germany's deadly new weapons. My mother, of course, laughed it off, just like she did in the Blitz. I think she had the same attitude as Churchill, who felt that the government should be honest with the people of Britain: that their fear and vicissitudes were part of the battle in France and they should be glad of the opportunity to share the dangers faced by the soldiers who were fighting out there. My mother was that type of patriot — if she was ever frightened by anything in the war, she certainly never let me know about it. Except losing her voice, that is; that certainly scared her. And, as one of the soldiers in Burma noted, she has never been very keen on thunderstorms!

The experience out in Burma had clearly made a big impression on Ma, and I don't think it was any coincidence that she and my father decided to buy Clayton Holt that summer of 1944. I like to think that this is really where I enter the story, for although I was not born until 1946, they clearly decided that they were serious about having a family and moving into what would become my first home — and what wonderful memories I have of it!

The end of Ma's tour in Burma was far from being the end of her involvement with the Burma boys — instead, it was the start of another story in which she would, in the spirit of her own song, fulfil the implicit promise she had made on her visit, and meet many of them again. A few years after the war, in

1951, the Burma Star Association was founded, creating an opportunity for veterans of the campaign to come together. Throughout its history, it has not only reunited veterans with one another; it has also helped to address their needs, along with those of their families and widows, through hardship funds and other welfare work. My mother was always treated as an honorary member of the Burma Star Association and she has had close ties with it through first of all Field Marshal Viscount Slim, as he became, and then, after his death in 1970, his son John. She was very proud, in 1985, to be awarded the War Medal and the Burma Star by Air Marshal Sir Bernard Chacksfield at the Royal Albert Hall. It was a particular honour because the Burma Star is a military medal, awarded to those who saw action there between 1941 and 1945. It has seldom been given to civilians.

My mother remained in touch with Slim for the rest of his life and followed his post-war career with interest. He was promoted after the war to the rank of field marshal and became the Chief of the Imperial General Staff — the head of the British Army — in 1949, succeeding Field Marshal Bernard Montgomery, who protested Slim's appointment by saying that he had told Sir John Crocker the job would be his. Prime Minister Clement Attlee's memorable reply was reported to be: 'Untell him!' Montgomery and Slim, by the way, are the only two Second World War generals to have statues in Whitehall — Slim's stands outside the Ministry of Defence. He remained as CIGS up until 1952, when he became Governor General of Australia. His classic account of the Burma campaign — *Defeat Into Victory* — was published in 1956. He retired in 1959 and moved back to Britain, where he sat on the boards of a number of companies; he held the title of Constable and Governor of Windsor Castle from 1964 up until his death in 1970.

He will always be best remembered, though, for his leadership in Burma, especially by the troops there who admired him so much. Antony Brett James, who fought in Burma, wrote: 'Bill Slim was to us a homely sort of general: on his jaw was carved the resolution of an army, in his stern eyes and tight mouth reside all the determination and unremitting courage of a great force. His manner held much of the bulldog, gruff and to the point, believing in every one of us, and as proud of the 'Forgotten Army' as we were.'

Ma went to many of the Burma reunions, which for decades were an annual event at the Royal Albert Hall, where she would often be introduced by Bill Slim before performing songs and talking to the veterans. I grew up going to these reunions with my mother and father, and I think it was these events that first really aroused my curiosity about what had happened in Burma. Ma has mentioned the story of Major Neville Hogan, who first stole a kiss from her when he was in hospital in Dibrugarh and repeated it sixty years later, at the 2004 reunion. It was such a poignant moment, as the article in the *Telegraph* below suggests:

Vera Lynn inspired a generation parted by war with her promise to 'meet again'. Yesterday it was fulfilled for one veteran of the Burma campaign when he exchanged kisses with the singer for the first time since their brief meeting in a field hospital 60 years ago.

Neville Hogan was 21 then and barely able to

stand. In addition to pneumonia, malaria and typhus, he had suffered a bullet wound to his shoulder during fierce fighting with the Japanese.

Dame Vera, as she would later become, stopped at his bedside during a tour of the hospital in eastern India and asked if there was anything she could do for him. 'I asked for a kiss,' said Mr Hogan, 'and she kindly obliged.'

She is now 87 and he 80 but Mr Hogan was no less flattered when the kiss was repeated during a reception at the Imperial War Museum marking the 60th anniversary of the battles of Imphal, Kohima and the Arakan.

Some 100 veterans of the battles, which raged throughout much of 1944, were present, representing one of the last great gatherings of members of the 14th Army before age takes its toll.

Despite their sacrifices, the men of the 14th were denied the fanfares accorded to troops in the European theatre, referring to themselves as the Forgotten Army.

Among those addressing the gathering was Countess Mountbatten of Burma, daughter of Earl Mountbatten, who commanded Allied forces in South East Asia. She told veterans: 'You definitely did not get your due at the end of the war. Well, you have got it now.'

The Burma campaign followed on from the shattering loss of Singapore in February 1942 and began with the longest retreat in British military history as Commonwealth forces fell back on India.

Only in 1944 did the tide truly turn when the 14th Army, which drew most of its troops from *the Indian Army, carried the battle into Burma under Gen. Sir William 'Bill' Slim. By then the British had learned the art of jungle warfare, in which disease and terrain posed as much of a threat as the enemy.*

Mr Hogan, who is half Irish and half Burmese Karen, was a Chindit, involved in operations behind enemy lines. 'The Japanese was a great soldier but he was cruel. We were killers but they were murderers.'

John Winstanley knew all about the ferocity of the Japanese. Now 84, he was a young company commander in the 4th Bn, the Royal West Kents during their defence of Kohima. 'We were out-numbered five to one and lost about half our men killed and wounded,' he said.

His company helped defend the tennis court on the Kohima perimeter, a surreal venue for brutal hand-to-hand fighting. 'The Japanese would attack at night, shouting and banging tins before charging in waves of banzai attacks.

'You had to admire their bravery but they sacrficed their status as human beings because of their behaviour. We loathed their brutality.'

''We'll Kiss Again' as Vera Lynn Meets her Chindit',
by Neil Tweedie (Telegraph, 22 April 2004)

At another reunion, she met up again with Ken Dix, who had been unable to see her when she spoke to him in hospital in Burma because his eyes were covered in bandages. In the 1950s, he became one of the first members of the North Surrey branch of the Burma Star Association. His son wrote a letter to Ma in which he mentioned that 'A few years ago at a

Remembrance service at Guildhall Cathedral he was absolutely delighted when you sat down at his table and chatted with him and some of his colleagues. This time he could see you!'

Neville Callaghan was a private in the 1st Battalion Northamptonshire Regiment in India, Ceylon and Burma between 1942 and 1944. He was not able to see my mother out in Burma because he was shot in the head twice by a Japanese sniper and, despite surviving, was then almost buried alive. He miraculously made it through this terrible experience, and, after first receiving treatment in Burma, was sent back to London for further rehabilitation at Queen Mary's Hospital in Roehampton. In 1945, Queen Mary's became a specialist centre for tropical diseases, and many of the Burma boys suffering from ailments including malaria, typhus and tropical infections were treated there after returning home. In 1945, when Ma was performing at the Shepherd's Bush Empire, some of the patients went to go and see her sing, and afterwards she signed programmes for several of them. Moving forward fifty years, in 1995 Ma was opening a fete at the Queen Alexandra Hospital Home in Worthing when Neville Callaghan turned up with his programme from that performance in Shepherd's Bush and asked her to sign it again, which of course she did. Perhaps the most amazing reunion was when the *This Is Your Life* team managed to find Gunner Fred Thomas, the soldier my mother had sung for in Dimapur when he was gravely ill. The show was made in 1957, thirteen years after their first meeting, and in much happier circumstances.

In the second edition of Ma's *This Is Your Life*, broadcast in December 1978, Lord Louis Mountbatten made an appearance. He soon after sent my Mother a letter in which he wrote:

I was very happy to be able to pay my tribute to all you have done, particularly for the Burma boys.
Yours affectionately,
Mountbatten of Burma

It may have been Mountbatten's appearance on television that had something to do with this next story.

You may remember Ern Mellet and Arthur Webberley, both of the 1st Somerset Company Regimental Police, who cheekily got to the front of the autograph queue at one of Ma's concerts in Burma when Ern feigned an injury. A sequel to this story came in 1979, when Ern sent his signed ten-rupee note to Lord Mountbatten and asked if he would autograph it next to my mother's signature. This Mountbatten did, sending it back with a letter asking if Ern had any spare rupee notes as he had none in his collection. The members of the Glastonbury Burma Star Association all contributed their spare notes and a full set was collected and mounted in a presentation wallet. They then arranged to visit Mountbatten's home, Broadlands, in September after he returned from Ireland to hand the wallet over. Although they did indeed visit Broadlands, the meeting never took place, as sadly Lord Mountbatten was killed off the coast of County Sligo on 27 August.

For Bert Thomas, who saw Ma sing in Burma, the memory remained with him for the rest of his life. In his 2012 letter to Ma he wrote:

Many years have passed since those days in Burma and I know, like me, you have passed your 90th birthday, but to those of us who were there at the time we shall always appreciate the effort you made to travel all those thousands of miles to entertain us, and to us you will always be our 'Forces' Sweetheart'.

One of the most emotionally affecting letters we received was from Christine Allen, the daughter of Stanley McDermott, who Ma had also visited in hospital, singing to him and one other man who did not survive. She wrote to my mother that 'we believe he stayed a little bit in love with you throughout his life'. The letter continues:

Dad suffered nightmares and flashbacks occasionally during his life, but very rarely spoke about the war. You were his proudest memory, and as the grandchildren (14) and great grandchildren (10 of them) came along, he never tired of telling them the story of 'The Forces' Sweetheart'.

He was eventually taken ill with cancer and left us at the age of 86. He wanted to be at home for the last week of his life but he was fighting to stay in his last few minutes. The room was packed with his family, so we all blessed him and told him to let go while we played your song 'White Cliffs of Dover' for him. Within minutes he slipped away with a smile and tears in his eyes. So God bless you, Dame Vera, for being there a second time when he needed you.

The fact that Ma had this profound and long-lasting effect on so many of the boys who served out there is, I think, the precise reason why she never quite got over the experience. There are so many stories of men who would talk of nothing else that happened in Burma to their families once they were home apart from seeing my mother singing or signing an autograph for them. She brought light into that dark jungle for so many of them. It was something that stayed with them for the rest of their lives, just as it has stayed with Ma for her whole life. John Sampson's daughter recalls: 'I can remember as a child Dad suffering with malaria which he first caught out in Burma; that was the only thing Dad told us about, apart from Vera Lynn.'

Another telling story along similar lines came from Alyson McGregor, whose father was a stand-in pianist for Ma, I assume in Calcutta, when her regular accompanist Len had an asthma attack.

My father, Mr Derek Daltry, who is now deceased, served in Burma during World War II but was always reluctant to talk of the experiences that he had endured during that time. However, he did talk affectionately of one experience where he had the pleasure in meeting you and in fact, due to the illness of your pianist, he was able to step in as a substitute and accompany you.

My father was a very experienced and talented pianist and he recalled that you had in fact given him a signed white £5 note which thanked him for standing in; he treasured this but unfortunately, this was lost during a fire much later on and he always spoke of his regret in losing this treasured possession.

We never forgot this story as it was one of the stories of that time he shared with his family, choosing to keep the horrific memories of combat to himself.

Sergeant Alwyn Denner was in 176 Squadron; his daughter wrote to Ma to tell her that her late father

would have been pleased, had he lived, to have written to you himself, with his own everlasting and unforgettable memories of having met you, whilst serving in India, including Burma. Although I am unable to extend to you all he would have remembered he recalled the pleasure and uplift you gave to the men during the extremely hard and difficult times, fighting for their country, whilst away from England and their loved ones, not knowing whether they would 'meet again'. Dad often recalled that you were afraid of thunderstorms.

There was an epitaph that was popular amongst the boys in Burma, and it is written on the monument that now stands in Kohima.

> *When you go home*
> *Tell them of us and say*
> *For their tomorrow*
> *We gave our today*

This simple sentiment reflects the fact that thousands of soldiers paid the highest price when they lost their lives in Burma. But I think we should remember that many of those fine young men who survived the experience of war never fully recovered from it. My mother has always supported the work of the Burma Star Association in its support of these men and their families.

My mother did not give up her today, but she understood those men who did. It was a tough but amazing experience for her; she says she would never have had such an opportunity were it not for the war. And she sees that as a positive thing — it allowed her to travel and see lots of different countries, cities like Cairo, Bombay and Calcutta, and unforgettable sights such as elephants in the wild and the pyramids. For a girl who had grown up in the East End of London, that was quite extraordinary at the time.

I've often thought of what that experience of being on the road for months must have been like for Ma. Her eye-watering itinerary meant that she was never in one place for long, and had very little time to herself, sometimes singing three times a day. Add to this the fact that she was travelling to places and climates she was completely unaccustomed to and visiting hospitals where men often had terrible injuries, and it is perhaps no surprise that she had to have some months off when she returned.

Of course she kept the good old British stiff upper lip, but the experience exhausted her, both mentally and physically. And I believe that the most draining thing of all was also the most thrilling and exciting — it was the fact that the men saw her as their salvation, and invested all their emotional energy in her visits. They whooped, they cheered, they hollered, they cried. She helped them express their emotions, which in the forces are often, necessarily, suppressed.

She helped them articulate their relationships with their sweethearts and families back home. She helped them remember England and gave them hope that they might one day return there. She gave them memories that would sustain them through more fighting and, for those who survived, would remain with them for the rest of their lives.

That is why I think she never got over it. And that is also why the story of her visit to Burma is such an extraordinary one that makes me so very proud of her. To undertake such a journey in her twenties, having only been abroad once before, and never having flown, was quite frankly amazing. She obviously felt very confident in her role and in the soldiers taking care of her, which of course they did marvellously. In fact the more I read about the actual battles and the arena of war in Burma, the more I am indebted to all the forces for their wonderful 'nanny' role!

Being forgotten was not just a problem of the time. My mother helped the Forgotten Army to feel that they were connected with home, that they were cherished and loved. But since 1944, the war in Burma, and the sacrifices made by the men who fought in it, has in general occupied a lesser role in the history books and the popular imagination compared with many other theatres of war. There are not many of the Burma boys left now, but I hope that this book goes some way to raising awareness of what they did out there and the suffering they had to endure, as well as celebrating the small but valuable contribution made by my mother to that conflict.

Recommended Further Reading

Annett, Roger, *Drop Zone Burma: Adventures in Allied Air-Supply 1943–45*, Pen & Sword Aviation, 2008

Holland, James, *Burma '44: The Battle that Turned the War in the Far East*, Bantam Press, 2016

Keane, Fergal, *Road of Bones: The Epic Siege of Kohima, 1944*, Harper Press, 2010

Latimer, John, *Burma: The Forgotten War*, John Murray, 2004

Lowry, Michael, *Fighting Through to Kohima: A Memoir of War in India and Burma*, Pen & Sword Military, 2008

Lyman, Robert, *Slim, Master of War*, Robinson, 2004.

Slim, Field Marshal Viscount, *Defeat Into Victory*, Cassell & Company, 1956

Acknowledgements

It has been a wonderful experience to talk to my mother about her journey of over seventy years ago and to look through all the letters she received both then and now. I know she would especially like to thank those wonderful families who have written in with stories about their brothers, fathers and grandfathers. And, of course, she would like to thank all the people in the services who looked after her during her time in India and Burma. She had faith that they would keep her safe — and they did!

Colonel John Slim, the 2nd Viscount Slim after his father, and his wife Elisabeth have been so helpful and supportive, and my mother and I would like to thank them both for their help with this book. Our families have been tied together for so many years now, and it is a wonderful friendship that we hope will last for many more years to come. In particular, I would like to thank Viscount Slim for allowing us to quote from his father's book *Defeat Into Victory*.

Our family's association with the Burma Star Association has also been an important one, and we would like to thank everyone who has worked there over the years, especially Phil Crawley, who has helped us with the book.

Although Len Edwards is no longer with us, it is important to remember the huge part he played, not only as my mother's pianist, but also as her friend. Unfortunately we have been unsuccessful in finding Len's family.

We would also like to thank everyone at the British Airways Heritage Centre and the RAF Museum. The Imperial War Museum collections have been essential for researching this book; they are a wonderful place to find out the stories of the men on the ground and I would like to thank Simon Offord at the Imperial War Museum as well as the copyright holders of all the following collections:

- Private papers of W Bratley (Documents. 1641)
- Private papers of Captain I A Wallace (Documents. 6985)
- Private papers of W N Elliot (Documents. 9800)
- Private papers of Mrs J Morton MBE (Documents. 3115)
- Private papers of Captain James Hough (Documents. 17391)
- The Second World War Memoir of Clifford Woodcock (Documents. 2197)

The newspaper archive at the British Library was also an important resource.

We would like to thank Pen & Sword Books for allowing us to quote from two wonderful books about the conflict in Burma: *Fighting Through to Kohima: A Memoir of War in India and Burma* by Michael Lowry; and *Drop Zone Burma: Adventures in Allied Air-Supply 1943–45* by Roger Annett.

Thank you to Ajda Vucicevic at Century, who commissioned this book and has been an enthusiastic and energetic supporter of it from the beginning, as well as her wonderful team for all their help. Thanks also to our literary agent, Andrew Gordon at David Higham Associates, who had faith in my idea and concept for the book. I would really like to acknowledge the hard work that Kevin Telfer has done on the book. He has done an incredible research job on both the historical and military side of the contents. He has followed the collated information that I gave him in the way of letters and photos etc., and also managed to pull together mine and my mother's voices in his narrative. Many thanks, Kevin; I wouldn't have been able to do this without you.

Lastly, I would like to thank my husband Tom, an RAF man himself, who knows quite a lot about being in a tight spot: I must give him a huge thank you for his patience and support whilst working on this book, which must have been somewhat trying at times. All my love, Tom. And of course, my other constant companion — Digby the dog, a little bundle of mischief who has been a source of constant amusement (and worry) throughout this whole project!

Last, but not least, I would like to mention the late Anita Nummo who was so instrumental in helping to get the letters and adverts out to all the newspapers, and helping me to reply to them all. Also for straining her eyes to read Ma's diary and typing it all out for me. Her help was invaluable in getting this book started.

Virginia Lewis-Jones, September 2017

Photographic Acknowledgements

- 'I have the feeling that this ride . . . ' © Alamy
- 'Without making any formal announcement . . . ' © Popperfoto/Getty Images
- 'The end of the tour in Burma was far from being the end . . . ' © Bill Lovelave/ANL/REX/Shutterstock
- 'Virginia, Tom and I at home . . . ' © Lucy Carnaghan Photography

All other photographs are author's own.

Every reasonable effort has been made to contact all copyright holders, but if there are any errors or omissions, we will insert the appropriate acknowledgement in subsequent printings of this book.

We do hope that you have enjoyed reading this large print book.

Did you know that all of our titles are available for purchase?

We publish a wide range of high quality large print books including:
Romances, Mysteries, Classics General Fiction Non Fiction and Westerns

Special interest titles available in large print are:
The Little Oxford Dictionary Music Book Song Book Hymn Book Service Book

Also available from us courtesy of Oxford University Press:
Young Readers' Dictionary (large print edition) Young Readers' Thesaurus (large print edition)

For further information or a free brochure, please contact us at:
Ulverscroft Large Print Books Ltd., The Green, Bradgate Road, Anstey, Leicester, LE7 7FU, England. Tel: (00 44) 0116 236 4325 **Fax:** (00 44) 0116 234 0205

Other titles published by Ulverscroft:

EDUCATED

Tara Westover

Tara Westover grew up preparing for the End of Days, hoping that when the World of Men failed, her family would continue on, unaffected. She hadn't been registered for a birth certificate. She had no school records because she'd never set foot in a classroom, and no medical records because her father didn't believe in doctors or hospitals. According to the state and federal governments, she didn't exist. As she grew older, her father became more radical, and her brother more violent. At sixteen, Tara decided to educate herself. Her struggle for knowledge would take her far from her Idaho mountains, over oceans and across continents, to Harvard and to Cambridge. Only then would she wonder if she'd traveled too far. If there was still a way home.

B. Keen